The Maltreated Child:

Finding What Lurks Beneath

The Maltreated Child:
Finding What Lurks Beneath

Steven G. Gray, Ph.D., A.B.Pd.N.

Photography by Sandi Evans
Illustrations by Tricia Lambert

Gray Neuropsychology Associates, Inc.
Arlington, Texas
Colorado Springs, Colorado

THE MALTREATED CHILD: FINDING WHAT LURKS
BENEATH

Published by Living Water Press
Colorado Springs, Colorado
For Permission/Information Address
1840 Deer Creek Road, Suite 103
Monument, CO 80132
Phone: 719.487.1760
Fax: 719.487.1755
e-mail: gray.matter@mindspring.com

Library of Congress Control Number: 2003116243
Cataloging-in-Publication Data
Gray, Steven G., 1953 –
The maltreated child: finding what lurks beneath

Includes biographical references and index
1. Psychology and Psychiatry   2. Neuropsychologic Testing
3. Adoptive/Foster Children   4. Child Rearing
I. Gray, Steven.   II. Title.

ISBN: 0-9746412-0-0

Printed in the United States of America

The Maltreated Child: Finding What Lurks Beneath

Table of Contents

Part IV Nautical Coordinates

Part V End Notes

Acknowledgements

To my Lord and Savior, Jesus Christ, who has afforded me countless blessings.

To my beautiful wife, Debbi, who has loved and supported me for over 22 years.

To my son, Forrest, of whom I am very proud.

To my late father and mother, Ed and Juanita Gray, who provided me with a loving, supportive home.

To my sister, Pam, who has always been a person of huge encouragement to me.

To my deceased aunt, Allene Gray, who instilled in me a love of learning.

To Dr. Bill Whitehouse, my cousin, surrogate uncle, and world-class role model.

To Jean LaPrade, an excellent grade-school teacher, who helped foster in me what it takes to complete a project.

To the late Bryan Duff, my esteemed high school English teacher, who engendered in me a love of writing.

To Dr. Charles Golden, whose brilliance and irascibility helped me learn how to think on my feet.

To Dr. Jack Dial, a good friend and invaluable mentor.

To Lyn Field, whose loyalty and administrative abilities helped make this book possible.

To Tricia Lambert, whose research efforts and many valuable suggestions allowed this book to become reality.

Introduction

How many times in 22 years of clinical practice have I heard the parent of a neglected/abused youth say, "You know, I **love** 'Billy,' but he is the *"Child from **Hell**"*?

Too many parents in our society have either thought this, or said this.

My prayer is that this book will inspire hope and provide effective options for the young person who appears *cursed*.

Steven Gray, Ph.D.
Colorado Springs, Colorado
April 2004

The Maltreated Child

Part I

Sea Hunt

Chapter 1

Anchor's Away:
The Neuropsychologic Evaluation

I thought I had hooked a big sailfish, of mammoth propor-tions...Come to find out, once I pulled everything up, it was only an old truck tire and rusted car fender, caught up on some heavy net-ting...

First impressions can be deceiving. Such is especially true when it comes to children and their behavior. As a grunt working down in the trenches of my private practice with young people over the past 20 years, I never cease to be amazed at how clouded and covert the true root causes of their aberrant behavior can be. One child looks ADHD (Attention Deficit Hyperactivity Disorder) on the surface, only to find he is suffering from a neurologic learning disorder and masked de-pression. Another angel appears Bipolar on the surface, only to dis-cover she is grappling with a Borderline Psychosis and RAD (Reactive Attachment Disorder).

What *is* a parent to do?

Fortunately, there *are* answers. It does involve a little adventure, going on a deep sea fishing voyage, with an experienced scuba diver who understands the undersea terrain and habitats of the various sea creatures. In order to help parents, the diver needs to know how to pull up the junk, *and* how to identify it. It is only after we discern that there is an old boot, a battered moss-covered golf club, and castaway cola bottle, that help can be found.

> The tests I use during a neuropsychologic evaluation allow me to *see into* the different areas of the brain... and assess the function of each.

Let me back up a bit though. I specialize in pediatric neuropsychology. In plain English, this is the diagnosis and treatment of various childhood/adolescent brain disorders. Inasmuch as we cannot peel back the skull to see how the brain is actually performing, I have to peek through various *windows* into the *gray matter,* to better understand what is actually going on inside. The tests I use during a neuropsychologic evaluation allow me to *see into* the different areas of the brain, if you will, and assess the function of each.

However, I did not *always* specialize in pediatric neuropsychology. First let me tell you a little of my own voyage.

Confessions of a Frustrated Psychotherapist

Remember the old *Bob Newhart Show* – the one where Dr. Robert Hartley, a Chicago based psychologist in private practice, worked with troubled adults, among whom was the irascible, irrepressibly cynical – yet somehow lovable – neurotic patient, Elliot Carlin?

That TV show in the mid to late 70s helped get me through my first 2 years of grad school – 7:30 p.m., Central Standard Time, Friday

11

nights. I really looked forward to it every week. But then, I didn't get *out* much.

Anyway, I was a Bob Hartley wannabe:

> have a nice suburban outpatient psychotherapy practice with adults,

> imbue keen and insightful verbal utterings to my patients.

Only one problem. I was lousy at conventional/Bob Hartley counseling.

Although highly analytical, I yearned for more closure in my work – a more finished *product*, if you will. Rarely did I see much by way of results via *the talking cure*, even after toiling with persons over a 1- to 2-year period in many instances.

As I mucked along for 5 years or so, primarily doing counseling with children and teens – a clinical focus in which I had been trained *and* an area of need at the time in the Dallas-Fort Worth Metroplex – I was miserable. And, to my mind, wholly ineffective.

I was a square peg trying to jam myself into a round hole.

> As I mucked along for 5 years or so, primarily doing counseling with children and teens...I was miserable. And, to my mind, wholly ineffective.

New Coordinates

Then I was introduced to the world of pediatric consulting. Well, one thing led to another: I undertook a 3-year post-doctoral clinical neuropsychology training program, began evaluating troubled children and teens via the use of neuropsychologic tests, and before long, I found myself really loving what I did. Not only that, but I began to primarily focus on maltreated foster and adoptive youth – who have very unique needs of their own.

Anyway, the purpose of these various tests is aimed at discovering what manner of brain-based disturbance constitutes the *root causes* of what ails highly difficult youth – and what, in turn, is driving their parents and families into acute renal failure.

I soon discovered that the moms and dads of these kiddoes were tremendously grateful for what it was I was doing: that is, giving them the primary root causes for why *their* foster/adoptive youngster was undergoing nuclear melt-down, often on a daily basis. For the first time in many cases, these parents now possessed *handles* for what was going on in their homes. Itches were being scratched.

So after 22 years in the mental health field, I have worked the last 11 of them almost exclusively with foster/adoptive kids and their families – doing consultations – and *not* doing traditional counseling. I now leave the specialized psychotherapy to the capable Dan Hughes, Greg Kecks, and Barbara Rilas of the world. The only exception is EEG Neurofeedback (see Chapter 15).

So, of what relevance is my journey to *you*?

(1) Well, if you happen to be a foster or adoptive parent who loves and cares for a difficult child, get a thorough evaluation done by a pediatric neuropsychologist. And do it **today**. The sooner the better. By knowing what the underlying root causes are, good counselors can then do *their* jobs much better. We are, then, that much closer to freeing up your kiddo to becoming all that she is meant to be, via the unique plan God has charted for her life. And that, for the Christian parent, is really what it's all about.

(2) Also, if your youth needs counseling, don't call me. *After all, Bob Hartley, I ain't*. But I *can* help you understand what is underneath your child's troubles. Then, once the root causes are pulled out of the channel, a viable treatment plan can be determined.

The Tip of the Iceberg

Consider a typical child who comes into my clinic. Let's say the young man, "Mark," is 10 years old. His presenting problems are wanton oppositionalism, chronic lying/stealing, lack of bonding, and academic underachievement to *beat the band*. He has become physically aggressive, furthermore demonstrating a penchant for smearing feces.

The lad was removed from his birth home at 3 years of age due to neglect and physical abuse. During the next 4 years, Mark lived with two different foster families. He was with his current family, in foster care, for 2 years. Adoption was consummated with them 1 year ago.

> His presenting problems are wanton oppositionalism, chronic lying/stealing, lack of bonding, and Academic Under-achievement to *beat the band*.

Mark exhibits the classic presenting symptoms among youth I see. In most cases, a parent has phoned in and said, "This is what my child is doing. My husband and I are ripping our hair out! What can we do, short of fleeing the country?!"

Most kiddoes, such as Mark, experience multiple symptoms, which have a bevy of various causes. They may be *mouthy*, hoarding food, sexually inappropriate, manipulative, bossy, and/or extremely moody.

> But while many of the children I work with have similar symptoms, does that mean they all have the same underlying diagnoses? No, not at all.

But while many of the children I work with have similar symptoms, does that mean they all have the same underlying diagnoses? No, not at all. The colossal *bugaboo* in diagnosing and working with young persons is first determining what is going on with **that** particular child. Any given youngster could have 6 or 7 underlying root causes, propping up his particular constellation of symptoms.

Thus, all we **see** from the top of the water is *the tip of the iceberg* – that is, the presenting problems. However, the bulk of the iceberg lies underneath the surface. Paul Harvey would tell us that below lies *the rest of the story* – in other words, the underlying root causes. Even though the youth I see can often look fairly uniform on the *outside*, in reality, many different factors are affecting their behavior, child by child. And if we try to treat them all the same, we fail miserably.

Combing the Ocean Floor

In essence, what I do every working day of my life is put on *scuba gear* and jump down into the murky waters. Next, I systematically search for the debris and grunge lying on any given youngster's *ocean floor*. I pull it up to the surface, see what it is, and then figure out what to do with it.

How do you help a young person or parent attack the symptom if you don't have a clear idea as to the actual *source* of the problem? You *can't*. If I have a pain in my right lower quadrant, I go to my esteemed internist, Dr. Steve Johnson of Fort Worth, Texas (aka: *Cowtown – Where the West Begins*). If he listens to me for about 30 seconds, and then miraculously declares that the cause of my pain is a diseased appendix, and furthermore that it must come out *today*, I am going to opine, "Time out! Let's talk this *over* a minute, porfa vor!"

> In essence, what I do every working day of my life is put on *scuba gear* and jump down into the murky waters.

But no competent physician would *ever* make a diagnosis that quickly, and in such a cavalier manner. There are way too many possible sources for my pain. Certainly, it could *be* my appendix – inflamed and about ready to blow. However, it *could* be an undetected tumor. It *could* be Irritable Bowel Syndrome. It *could* be the bad Mexican food I had last night. (By the way – not to brag – but among local Tex-Mex restaurants, I am affectionately known as *The Amazing El Consumo*.)

But I digress. At any rate, the learned *Dr. J* is *not* going to make a snap diagnosis based on 30 seconds' worth of history. He will order tests. Additional questions will be asked. X-rays might be taken. My physician is going to do his homework.

> I must do **my** *homework* to discover what sort of refuse lies on his ocean floor.

It is no different with a child who is entrusted to me. I must do **my** *homework* to discover what sort of refuse lies on his ocean floor. This is something for which I have a real passion. I love what I do. I love getting up in the morning, helping children and parents find practical interventions to the problems they face.

Family Destination – The Bermuda Triangle

For example, perhaps a young lady, "Heather," has been to 3 Residential Treatment Centers (RTCs), 4 psychiatric hospitals, with a total of 6 different therapists over the last 4 years. Nevertheless, every one in the family is still on the verge of a nervous breakdown. They are living in a perpetual Bermuda Triangle.

I ask Mom if Heather has clinical records from these places. The usual reply is, "Yes, I'll send them over." Soon thereafter, a Mac truck pulls up in front of my clinic, resembling some sort of FBI sting operation – crates and boxes of documents galore. It takes a forklift to get them all in.

Even so, I need to do **my** *homework* in getting these all read. Without such, and short of a thorough neuropsychologic evaluation by me, I am doing nothing more than blindly throwing darts inside a tawdry Irish seaside tavern.

Why do I *do* this? Why get my hands dirty in all the grime and filth that lies beneath the waterline? The *reason* is because I need to find out, as precisely as possible, what the underlying root causes are (there's that term again) for Heather. And, I want to show the *parents* what is underneath the symptoms she is displaying. Moreover, I want to give them the information *they* need to determine what is best for *Heather*.

The good news here is that the ocean floor *can* in most instances be cleaned up – even if we are talking major toxic spill. The first trick is finding out what exactly needs to be flushed out. The thoroughness of the testing ensures that we do not just scoop up a little off the top, and head back to the beach house. Rather, *Lloyd Bridges-ilk* scuba gear allows me to swim down to the ocean floor, where the contents can be carefully gathered up, brought back up to the surface, and systematically nuked – one by *one*.

The good news here is that the ocean floor *can* in most instances be cleaned up – even if we are talking major toxic spill.

So, let the dive begin!

Chapter 2

Outfitting Our Gear for the Dive: Testing Day

The typical scenario is this, using our man, Mark, as an example. Adoptive mom calls *May-Day* into our clinic. Mark is making life miserable for everyone at home and school. So, we first listen to her description of what all is occurring. Then an appointment is set up for her son to come in.

Diving Class

On the appointed date, Mark will spend the better part of the day at our clinic. In most cases, the testing will require approximately 6 hours. We start at 9:00 a.m. – generally finishing all procedures around 3:30 p.m. There are several breaks along the way, as well as a lunch period. During said breaks, the child can visit our internationally renown 4-Star snack room, listed prominently within *The Mobil Travel Guide.*

For lunch, the youth often goes out-to-eat that day with his mom – a treat most youngsters love! Usually the testing is on a school day; so in addition, he gets to miss a day in the classroom – praise *God*!

Thus, all in all, I am the best thing since sliced bread to these young people. Incidents of test-balking by a kiddo are indeed rare!

As for the procedures we use to measure Mark's brain function, almost all possess a decided *game-like* aura. Youth typically enjoy the various tests we give, and leave having had a wonderful time during our deep-sea fishing expedition. In fact, most youngsters hate to leave, frequently expressing the desire to remain, "play some *more*," and spend the night with us (because, after all, we **do** sleep there in the clinic, don't we?).

Denizens of the Deep

Some of the assorted sea life and *gar-báge* (from the French) I am looking for with each youngster include:

(a) Overall Cognitive Capacity – to see if there are any areas and/or functions of the brain which are not processing information correctly – causing problems in school, home, etc

(b) Intellectual Function (both *Paper IQ* as well as genetic/God-given IQ)

(c) Academic Skills (reading, writing, arithmetic, etc)

(d) Academic Underachievement (discovering the root causes of an otherwise bright youngster's poor academic grades)

(e) Attention Deficit Hyperactivity Disorder

(f) Basic Personality Temperament

(g) Stress Proneness/Emotionality (possible anxiety/nervousness, stress-related physical ailments, *masked* depression, etc)

(h) Medication Options

(i) Reactive Attachment Disorder

(j) Borderline Conditions of Childhood/Adolescence

(k) Bipolar Disorder

(l) Character Pathology

Current technology (the range of available neuropsychologic tests) allows us to scuba dive with anyone from 4 years of age up through young adulthood.

As to specifics, it is important that Mark get a good night's sleep prior to testing, as well as having eaten a good breakfast before coming in. Upon arrival, the pediatric neuropsychometrist spends 15 to 20 minutes visiting/conversing with the child or teen to establish rapport, prior to beginning the first procedure.

Also during the morning, I or one of my staff will conduct a parent interview in an adjacent office while the youngster is testing. Part of what helps to discover what gunk is on the ocean floor is provided via information regarding family of origin (FOO) – including any known mental health disorders among blood relatives, gestational/developmental/medical history, etc. While I know in cases of foster and adoptive children, little of this information may be available, I *do* try to gather as much early history as possible.

In essence, the contents of a pediatric neuropsychologic exam are comprised of: (1) history; (2) behavioral observations; and (3) test data of the kiddo. For a thorough assay of the ocean floor, all **three** are crucial.

In addition, I look at current academic achievement, social and interpersonal behavior, the sleep/wake cycle, appetite, mental status, and any other specific concerns that you as the parent may have regarding your child or teen.

Final Pieces of Gear

So, our neuropsychometrist does the morning testing, broken into 3 or 4 sessions. As mentioned above, several breaks are scattered throughout the day in order that fatigue does not become a factor – as well as the lunch period (you may either send a sack lunch – Mark simply eats with us – or take him out-to-eat, whichever is preferable).

During the afternoon sessions, the psychometrist performs more tests. Then we conduct a clinical interview with the child. Again, many breaks occur so that the youngster becomes neither tired nor stressed.

In my 20 years of private practice – at this writing – I can literally count on one hand the number of youth who have been uncooperative such that testing could not occur! Bizarre, huh? It truly is amazing how even the kids with the very *worst* behavior/mucked up ocean floors are almost always on their best behavior with *us*. And, don't worry, parents, these facades do **not** throw us off, in terms of our findings! Part of our training is to *see through* their underwater subterfuge.

> In my 20 years of private practice...I can literally count on one hand the number of youth who have been uncooperative such that testing could not occur!

Medications: Fresh or Salt Water?

Most parents ask if their child should be off his medications for the day of testing. Actually, it is of greater value if the youngster is *on* his usual psychotropic regimen. So if the youth is on any medications, he should go ahead and take them as prescribed. Moreover, it is crucial that any noon dosage (as in the case of Ritalin, Adderall, Dexedrine, Cylert, Dextrostat, etc) be brought on the day of testing. Basically, **all** medicines should be taken as prescribed.

The evaluation will help us determine if Mark's current meds are doing the job for which they are intended. Moreover, from the results, we can ascertain, in conjunction with the prescribing physician, whether dosages need to be titrated up or down, or whether the youngster even *needs* a particular agent he is currently on, or *not*.

The only exception to this will be in the case of a youth whose parents wish to clarify whether an ADHD exists. In these instances we will ask to assess the child *au naturalé* (again, from the French) – i.e., off his psychostimulant meds on the day of exam with us. This way, we can accurately judge whether ADHD is one piece of whatever refuse lies on the bottom of the channel.

Summary

So herein is the raw-realism description of a day at *Sea World* with us. We try to keep it fun for the youngsters. And for me, well, I love the smell of the salt air, the ocean mist in my face. I like even *more* the day we get to do the staffing/feedback session with the parents. Here is where we reveal to them whatever sorts of malevolent sea-life are lurking down in the bowels of the gulf for their son or daughter. Then, with underlying root causes dredged up for us to *see*, we can formulate an effective toxic spill clean-up.

Chapter 3

Sharing the Captain's Log:
The Parent Feedback Session

Once the scuba dive is over, then comes an analysis of all the muck dredged up from the depths. Given that I didn't just get off a rickety rowboat, having worked for many years with troubled youth, I have seen virtually all manner of crappola brought up from the ocean floor. Little really surprises me anymore. But let me assure you that along with the debris causing the behavioral mayhem, there are also the God-given qualities which make your child unique. Part of my ministry, is *finding* them, and helping you, the parent, nurture them.

Hauling in the Net

Once the tests are completed, I score/tabulate them, and then the analysis of the results ensues. It is important that these procedures are understood in light of: (1) my eye-ball observations of the youngster; and (2) developmental/medical history. You, her parents, have already given me: Heather's medical history, vegetative signs (such as wake/sleep cycle, appetite, etc), academic status, and interpersonal skills. All are important factors in determining the root causes of the problem(s). In brief, a *shot-gun marriage* takes place between Heather's test data and her background (what we shrinks call *history*).

It takes approximately 10 working days after the date of the evaluation for all results and findings to be assessed and assayed. In addition, a thorough report detailing the youngster's presenting problems, history, test results, conclusions, diagnoses, and recommendations is generated. I give parents a copy of my detailed report. This is unedited – unsanitized. Such can also be provided to physicians, counselors, the school, or whomever you choose. But, *no* results go anywhere without your written consent.

> ...a *shot-gun marriage* takes place between Heather's test data and her background...

Then, usually a couple of weeks post-evaluation, I sit down with Mom and Dad for a feedback/staffing session. I sit in the middle, between them, on the large couch in my office. We go over all the results, test by test, in a relaxed, unhurried fashion. This session usually takes 2½ to 3 hours. Such allows plenty of time for any and all questions.

Most of the various procedures have *no-brainer* graphs that easily reveal, from a visual standpoint, what is happening with your youngster. I show these *to* you. All findings, diagnoses, and recommendations are included in the detailed report. It is also fine for parents to audiotape the feedback session, should you so desire. Moreover, grandparents, counselors, or anyone else you wish, may attend this session.

Charting the Course

Once the test results are presented, we go down the cafeteria line of various options for treatment/habilitation – tailored specifically for your foster, adoptive, or birth child. I do my best to present the pros and cons for each possible way we can attack the underlying root causes for what is going on with Heather.

By the way, I do not see it as *my* right to cram broccoli down the throat of either George Bush, Sr. – or a parent, if that parent abhors broccoli. Hence, I do not *lobby* for a particular medication, type of therapy, or any other course of action for your child. My job, as I see it, is to be the *very best consultant* I can be for you – serving up the findings on your youngster – to you the parent. After all, no one knows your kiddo better than you do!

> I do my best to present the pros and cons for each possible way we can attack the underlying root causes for what is going on with Heather.

Choices at SeaWorld

My approach is to offer up all the various methods that have been shown to help youngsters with the type of neuropsychologic profile *your* kiddo possesses. During the staffing, I answer questions, giving you the benefit of my years groping around on the bottom of the sea. But, God has not given *me* the right to make decisions regarding your child. He has given this to *you*! But I will assist you in every way I can.

> My approach is to offer up all the various methods that have been shown to help youngsters with the type of neuropsychologic profile *your* kiddo possesses.

Thus, what happens is you end up doing a Vulcan *mind-meld* from what you hear from me – incorporating that with prayer, along with wise counsel obtained from others. Then, and only then, are you ready to choose which specific courses of action to take pursuant to your son or daughter – to cleanse out the undersea muck.

Medications: Fresh or Salt Water? Part II

Together, we look at all manner of medications, for example, checking out pros and cons. Some parents are very wary of psychotropics for a child – especially *their* child. Others are very *pro* medication. And then there are those who are simply not sure *how* they feel about medication for youth. Such ambivalence is very common among parents. And, you know what? It is fine to be unsure. If you possessed all the answers, you would not need *me*. And if I possessed **all** the answers, I would be in Heaven's tenor section, singing with the saints.

Perhaps however you have seen other youth, similar to your own, who have done well on a particular medication. And, you think, "Wow, I would like for *my* child to improve also; but you know, I really am *scared* of giving these types of medicines to a youngster." So during the parent feedback session, we take our time, carefully talk through the pros and cons for the entire tackle box of recommendations, be it behavioral changes, increased academic motivation, disciplinary strategies, psychotropic options – *whatever*. My goal and expectation is that your youth will find light at the end of the tunnel – regardless of *whichever* recommendations you decide upon.

> ...no earthly individual knows the child better than you, the parents.

Again, to completely run the seahorse into the sand, my firm notion is that despite the thoroughness of the neuropsychologic evaluation, no earthly individual knows the child better than you, the parents. Therefore, I do not believe that any recommendations for a kiddo should be *force-fed* to parents. It is *your* right to choose which, if any, of the various recommendations I provide. But now you have the *handles* to make these decisions – medications or no.

There *is* Hope

Bottom line as I see it – my job is put on my scuba gear, go down and thoroughly comb the ocean bottom, scavenging for the underlying root causes of *whatever* symptoms are menacing your child or teen. Then, I *resurface,* hauling up and revealing to you whatever I find, thoroughly discussing the various options that can clean up your youngster's marine floor. My mission is to show you, the parents, each piece of seaweed, beer bottle, rusted hubcap – or *whatever* – serving to pollute your precious kiddo.

...in every situation, there *is* hope!

My goal, then, is for you to gain a thorough and accurate picture of your youth. In keeping with my philosophy, I do not *sugarcoat* anything. But at the same time, I also do not catastrophize anything. Because in every situation, there *is* hope! And that is what we are all looking for – *hope*, and a battle plan.

Summary

Doing what I do, I have had the opportunity to follow scores of severely disturbed youth – serially, from the age of 5 or 6 up to their late teens/early 20s – having been able to test them 6 or 7 times from age 5 to 20ish. The oft miraculous outcome is that most of these kiddoes, who struggled mightily during their growing-up years, were and *are* able to overcome their childhood challenges and become productive/well-adjusted adults. I have seen it over and over and over again. Currently though, as parents, you are in the best position to make the best choices for your child today. And, I'll help you gather the data you need to *make* those decisions. As bleak as it seems now – don't give up. It's merely time to bring in the Marines. So, let's **do** it!

Chapter 4

The Dive Map:
Brain Regions and Functions

The human brain is truly a marvel. Reflecting upon the abilities of our *gray matter* is like admiring a beautiful bed of coral reef. The design, the capability, and the capacity of this organ are amazing. The sophistication of the cerebral cortex differentiates man from all other creatures. It is ¼ inch thick, surrounding the entire cerebrum. The cortex allows humans to perform higher level activities such as speaking, reasoning, judgment, mathematics, planning, reading, etc.

The brain is responsible not only for our cognitive processes but also our emotions, volition, behavior, and dreams. It is the command center of our physical bodies; yet it also somehow contains the core of our soul – what makes me *me* and you *you*. The brain coordinates a vast amount of information, sending and receiving more messages in a day than can be counted.

*Cayman Brac is in the Western Caribbean, 480 miles south of Miami.

Anatomy of the Brain

Inasmuch as it has been more years than we probably care to admit since most of us sat in high school biology class, let me briefly review a little bit of anatomy.

The brain is protected on the outside by the skull. Of course, research has shown teenagers' skulls to be at least 2 inches thicker than that of the average adult! Such usually thins back to normal during their 20s, praise God. Underneath the skull, also offering protection of the gray matter, are three thin layers of membranes called the meninges. Cerebrospinal fluid flows between the inner and middle layers of the meninges serving as shock absorbers, if you will, in the event of a blow to the head.

Underneath the membranes are the three main portions of the brain: the cerebrum, the cerebellum, and the stem. The cerebrum is the largest section. It controls our thinking. It is where we process all kinds of information. This is the seat of government for many of our voluntary actions. The cerebrum breaks down into two layers. The outermost layer (the cortex) is known as gray matter, and the inner portion (the sub-cortex) is composed of white matter.

The cerebellum, on the other hand, is tucked under the cerebrum at the back of the head. It controls balance and coordination. The cerebellum is able to take gross motor movements organized in the cerebrum and fine-tune them into the precise movements required by, say, a surgeon, artist, or sprinter.

The third region is the brain stem. This is basically the stalk holding up the brain, connected to the base of the head, leading down into the spinal cord. It is composed of three parts: the medulla oblongata, pons, and midbrain. Together these control involuntary actions such as digestion, breathing, heart rate, etc – regulating our vital functions.

The Cerebrum

The cerebrum is divided into two hemispheres, joined together by the corpus callosum – sort of the brain's *50 yard-line*. Think of the corpus callosum as the *delivery man,* passing messages back and forth between the two halves, allowing them to communicate.

Do you remember the pictures of the brain in your high school biology book? It is always depicted as a wrinkled mass, similar in appearance to a very bloated walnut. All those hills and valleys maximize the actual surface area of the brain, allowing it to fit inside our skull.

In general, and for most people, the right hemisphere governs the left side of the body, in terms of motor function (see Figure 4.1). It is often described as the *artistic* side of the brain – the site for creative thinking, as well as intuitive responses. Our musical/artistic skills (or lack thereof) originally come from this region. However, once a musical skill (e.g., playing the trumpet) is learned, this ability is thought to shift to the left hemisphere, at least in part – inasmuch as playing the trumpet has now taken on a distinct aspect of *language* (primarily a function of the left hemisphere). The right side of the brain is also the headquarters of visual-perceptual skills (e.g., finding our car in a crowded parking lot, or making sense out of an architect's blue-print, etc).

> Think of the corpus callosum as the *delivery man,* passing messages back and forth between the two halves, allowing them to communicate.

The left side of the cerebrum, correspondingly, controls the right side of the body motorically (i.e., right arm and right leg). For approximately 90% of us, this side reigns over language skills: speech, writing, word identification, receptive/expressive language (speaking), etc (see Figure 4.2). This side is also responsible for step-by-step thinking, thus gaining the reputation for being the *logical* side of the brain.

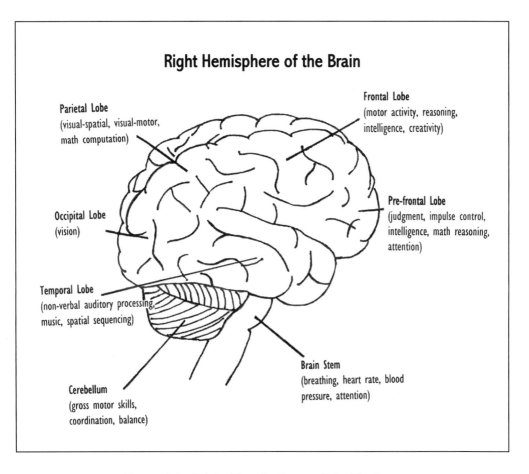

Figure 4.1 Right Hemisphere of the Brain

Both hemispheres of the cerebrum are composed of the same five lobes: pre-frontal, frontal, temporal, parietal, and occipital. The frontal region is located behind the forehead, with the pre-frontal portion serving as *point-man* (*directly* behind the forehead). The temporal lobes are the areas of the brain under the temples. The parietal regions are near the back of the boat, with the occipital located at the *very* back of the brain, just above the cerebellum.

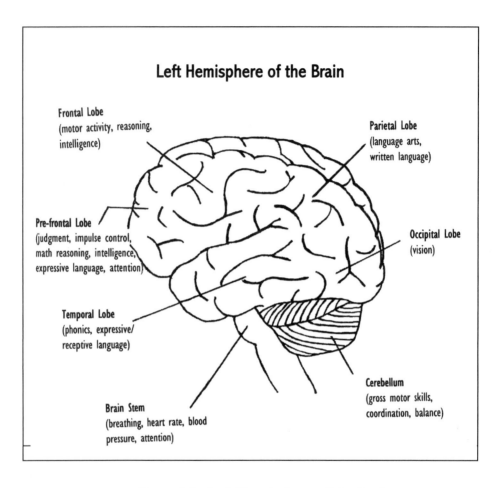

Left Hemisphere of the Brain

Frontal Lobe
(motor activity, reasoning,
intelligence)

Parietal Lobe
(language arts,
written language)

Pre-frontal Lobe
(judgment, impulse control,
math reasoning, intelligence,
expressive language, attention)

Occipital Lobe
(vision)

Temporal Lobe
(phonics, expressive/
receptive language)

Cerebellum
(gross motor skills,
coordination, balance)

Brain Stem
(breathing, heart rate, blood
pressure, attention)

Figure 4.2 Left Hemisphere of the Brain

Each lobe is responsible for different functions within the brain. It is to these five regions toward which I pay particular homage as I perform neuropsychologic testing. The pre-frontal areas are responsible for abstract reasoning, common sense reasoning, impulse control, the ability to hold off or delay instant gratification, etc. It is also here that inattention problems frequently surface (as well as in a clump of cells within the brain stem – the Reticular Activating System, or RAS).

The posterior frontal lobes direct motor movement. As stated, the right frontal controls the left side of the body motorically, while the left frontal operates the right side – motorically.

Vision is coordinated by the occipital lobes. These help us identify or make sense out of the objects we see.

The parietal regions are particularly attuned to incoming sensory information, including complex visual-spatial messages. This information enables us to understand our environment with regard to size, shape, and depth.

Auditory processing occurs within the temporal lobes, enabling us to decode sounds. It also houses some important areas for understanding language and the formation of speech. In addition, it is the primary area within the cortex responsible for memory.

Messaging

Scientists have made great strides in the last 50 years, understanding the brain and how it works. The cells which make up our central nervous system are called neurons. Each one has a nucleus. Unique to the neurons are the axons and dendrites branching off the nucleus. An axon is a long projection off the nucleus which carries messages to another neuron. A dendrite is a branched filament of the cell which brings impulses *into* the it (see Figure 4.3).

Messages passed along from cell to cell are done so via electrical and chemical transmissions. One cell's axons reach out toward another neuron's dendrites. They do not actually touch one another.

The microscopic space between them is known as the synapse (see Figure 4.4). In the tiny gaps are chemicals known as neurotransmitters which help pass the messages along, allowing the messages to *jump* across the synapse. A medication that Mark or Heather might be taking helps restore efficiency in neurotransmitter function within the millions of miniscule gaps within the brain.

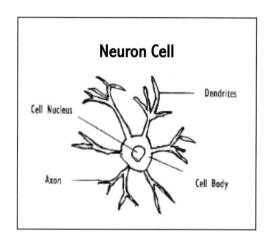

Figure 4.3   Neuron Cell

Neurons pass information in one of two forms: *on* or *off*. The neurons string together messages, all operating at either *on* or *off*. With all the different cells firing impulses, complicated messages can be sent.

Cells are classified by what job they perform. Sensory (or afferent) neurons are the ones which carry messages from our sensory organs (eyes, ears, skin, etc) through the spinal cord and on to the brain. Motor (or efferent) neurons carry transmissions from our brain to the rest of the body (arms, feet, face, etc). A third type of neuron is called connectors (or interneurons). These communicate between sensory and motor neurons.

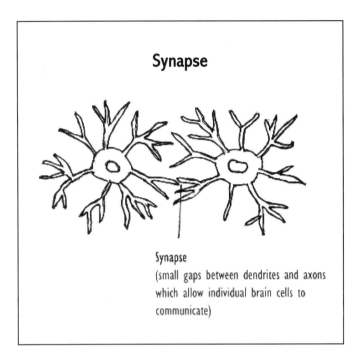

Synapse

Synapse
(small gaps between dendrites and axons
which allow individual brain cells to
communicate)

Figure 4.4 Synapse

Hot Spots

Once the refuse from the bottom of Mark's ocean floor is pulled up, we then seek to identify the *latitudinal and longitudinal coordinates* from which the trouble comes. There are a few disorders we have been able to *place*. For example, for many youth who possess organically-driven explosive disorders, such usually stem from abnormal electrochemical firing within the temporal lobes.

We also know that a great deal of behavioral mayhem flows from the bilateral pre-frontal regions. Think of the pre-frontal region as the CEO of the brain – collecting information, synthesizing/analyzing it, and then making a decision.

Some kiddoes have a benevolent CEO, such as a Dr. James Dobson of Focus On the Family (currently chairman of the board at Focus). Others possess a malevolent CEO, such as that of pre-scandal Enron. My job is to help devise a treatment plan for a child to turn an *Enron* into a *Focus On the Family*.

This area, the pre-frontal cortex, is a *hot spot* for potential emotional/behavioral pandemonium, rather like unto the Gaza Strip of the brain. Stemming from here are the behavioral syndromes such as impulse control disorders, ADHD, Conduct Disorder, as well as Oppositional Defiant Disorder, etc.

Fortunately, the pre-frontal region of the human brain, most responsible for overall capacity of what a youngster ultimately can achieve vis-à-vis executive function (Enron or Focus on the Family), does not anatomically and physiologically mature for most persons until their mid to late 20s, or even until age 30ish. Thus, any

> This area, the pre-frontal cortex, is a *hot spot* for potential emotional/behavioral pandemonium, rather like unto the Gaza Strip of the brain.

given child still has much time left for optimization of brain development via his pre-frontal lobes.

Consequently, we should see gradual pre-frontal development throughout the young person's teen years, leading *up* to age 25 or so, and even possibly to age *30* – assuming we have a carefully crafted and operational treatment plan in place. Brain injury is about the only reason an adolescent would digress rather than progress in brain development.

Summary

Understanding the various regions of the brain and their functions is one of the first steps in determining what is tormenting a particular young person. Next, we need to match this up with the child's history and behavioral problems. Such taken together gives us an excellent idea of what is menacing a certain kiddo. We can then determine if the behavior is likely stemming from a masked depression, ADHD, a learning disability – or a tainted seafood platter of all **three**.

The Maltreated Child

Part II

20,000 Leagues Under the Sea

Chapter 5

Sonar:
IQ Considerations

O. K. My scuba gear is now on, and I'm peering under the surface of the deep. One of the first things I look for is the contour of the ocean floor itself. Am I somewhere in the North Sea off the coast of Ireland – *or* am I descending down to the Great Barrier Reef in the Land Down Under? Well, I'm going to follow the sights to help me get my bearings. Extending the metaphor to troubled youth and what lurks beneath the water-line of *her* mind, one of the first pieces of data I look at is the *Paper IQ* (that which is determined by actual scores off IQ tests), as well as the God-given/genetic intelligence (a far more telling number in many respects, derived from multiple tests). Both the *Paper IQ* and Heather's God-given/genetic intelligence are discussed below.

The IQ Test

This is a tool that helps us measure a child's ability to successfully negotiate his environment. However, it is important to remember that the utility of an IQ score is limited by the clinical acumen of the person looking at it. There is a danger of someone working with our youth who does not know the ins and outs of how to make sense regarding this type of score.

That is, do we take an IQ number at face value? If not, what are we to make of it? As we will learn here in a moment, with youngsters hailing from backgrounds of neglect and/or abuse, there are certain unwritten laws that govern how we interpret an individual IQ score. But, I'm getting ahead of myself. Let's first look at some of the more basic aspects of intelligence testing.

The following table lists the standard parameters of IQ measurement:

IQ Score Ranges

130 +	Very Superior	70 - 79	Borderline Mentally Retarded
120 - 129	Superior	55 - 69	Mild Mentally Retarded
110 - 119	Above Average	40 - 54	Moderate Mentally Retarded
90 - 109	Average	25 - 39	Severe Mentally Retarded
80 - 89	Low Average	<24	Profoundly Mentally Retarded
	(*Slow Learner*)		

Figure 5.1   IQ Score Ranges

IQ scores are reflected in the typical bell curve. Average range scores (90 to 109) apply to roughly 50% of the general population. Scores from 80 to 89 comprise what commonly are described as the *Slow Learner* range. IQs within the 70s constitute the Borderline MR range (sometimes simply called the *Borderline range*). IQs of 69 and below typically constitute the MR range. On the other end of the continuum, IQs of roughly 130 and above fit into the *Gifted and Talented* range.

Low IQs

Factors which may contribute to a low score on an intelligence test are: genetics, lack of environmental enrichment, in utero drug/alcohol exposure, and traumatic brain injury. IQ often follows a genetic course. Typically, the higher the intelligence of the parents, the brighter the child. The converse is true as well. Consequently, if a youth's IQ is dramatically different from the parents' (particularly lower), we know to look for possible factors which might explain the difference – such as brain trauma, in utero drug/alcohol exposure, and/or severe neglect.

There are three main pieces of nuclear fallout from Fetal Alcohol Exposure (FAE), or the more pronounced Fetal Alcohol Syndrome (FAS). Such include neurologic learning disabilities, ADHD, and brain dysfunction. How bad is the organic disturbance going to *be*? It most often depends on the amount of alcohol and drugs the mother was consuming during pregnancy.

Even so, it has been my experience that around 33% of children with in utero exposure will come out clean as a whistle on neuropsychologic testing, in spite of the mother having been on truckloads of cocaine and massive alcohol during pregnancy. It makes no rational sense that any child's brain could emerge from such unscathed. Here, we simply rejoice in the grace of God.

> Even so, it has been my experience that around 33% of children with in utero exposure will come out clean as a whistle on neuropsychologic testing...

Lastly, brain injury can also affect the IQ of a youngster. Should this unfortunate circumstance occur, rehabilitation is a key ingredient in restoring cognitive capabilities – usually via neurologic compensation – i.e., an undamaged area of the brain *taking over for* the affected region. Another tool, EEG Neurofeedback (see

Chapter 15), can also be a God-send in restoring normal organic function to damaged areas.

Wechsler Intelligence Scale for Children - III

To measure the youth's functional intellect, I use the *Cadillac* of IQ tests: the Wechsler Intelligence Scale for Children – III (WISC-III) for youngsters, ages 6 to 16, or the Wechsler Adult Intelligence Scale – III (WAIS-III) for youth, ages 17 and up. Among kiddoes 4 to 5 years of age, I use the Wechsler Pre-School and Primary Scale of Intelligence – III (WPPSI-III).

All three tests are similar in structure and roughly measure the same proficiencies. For our purposes here, we'll use the WISC-III for our base of discussion. The Stanford-Binet is another good IQ test – think of it as a Lexus. The Kaufman Battery could be a BMW.

At any rate, the WISC-III divides off into two general categories: (1) Verbal Scale subtests; and (2) Performance Scale subtests. Each renders an IQ number – the *VIQ* (Verbal), and *PIQ* (Performance). These two scores, taken together, constitute the Full Scale IQ (or *FIQ*) of the child.

The Verbal section is composed of tests oriented toward Heather's ability to understand and communicate orally for the most part. The Performance section (which I wish would have been labeled *Visual-Motor IQ*, for clarity's sake) on the other hand measures visual-motor and visual-spatial abilities – involving hands-on tasks (constructing complex puzzles, analyzing pictures, arranging colored blocks in certain geometric patterns, etc).

If the WISC-III PIQ is *lower* than the VIQ, such may constitute a marker of depression....

Generally, in boys, as well as *some* pre-teen girls, PIQ is usually higher than the VIQ, at least by a little bit. If the WISC-III PIQ is *lower* than the VIQ, such may constitute a marker of depression (except in cases of right hemispheric compromise).

A significant split between the PIQ and VIQ (16 points or more) can also denote subtle brain dysfunction. If the VIQ is weak, we generally are looking at left hemisphere involvement – if a low PIQ, right hemispheric (or possible depression). For you masochists out there, see Chapter 21 for more technical information on this test.

Verbal Subtests

Subtest	Measures	May Reveal Problems In
*Information	fund of stored knowledge	impoverished background, or poor verbal memory
*Similarities	abstract reasoning	left pre-frontal region
+*Arithmetic	numerical operation skills	attention/concentration; math skills
*Vocabulary	generic verbal ability	generic left hemisphere
*Comprehension	common sense reasoning	left pre-frontal region
+Digit Span	auditory attention span	attention/concentration

*Can be used to estimate God-given Verbal IQ for a youth.
+ ADHD-Sensitive Subtests

Figure 5.2   WISC-III Verbal Subtests

WISC-III Verbal Subtests

From various Verbal Scale subtests off the Wechsler, along with road-signs from the Woodcock-Johnson Revised (see Chapter 6), and Test of Auditory Discrimination (see Chapter 21), a child's genetic VIQ can be estimated. The VIQ portion is composed of 6 subtests which are briefly described in the table above. Again, for a somewhat meatier discussion of the various WISC-III Verbal subtests, see Chapter 21.

WISC-III Performance Subtests (aka: *Visual-Motor* Subtests)

The other five subtests comprise the Performance section of the Wechsler. (Once more, I prefer the term *Visual-Motor* section.) These tests are more sensitive to right hemispheric function of the brain, for 90% of people walking around out there. Chapter 21 also discusses the five WISC-III Performance subtests in a bit more detail.

Performance Subtests

Subtest	Measures	May Reveal Problems In
+Picture Completion	visual attention to detail	visual/attention concentration
+Coding	visual attention	visual/attention concentration
Picture Arrangement	pictorial sequencing	right temporal region
Block Design	complex visual-spatial skills	right parieto-occipital region
Object Assembly	complex visual-spatial skills	right parieto-occipital region

+ADHD-Sensitive Subtests

Figure 5.3 WISC-III Performance Subtests

WISC-III Attention-Sensitive Subtests

As stated above, the WISC-III has four individual subtests which are sensitive to attention/concentration parameters: Arithmetic and Digit Span (both *auditory* attention), along with Picture Completion and Coding (both *visual* attention). Looking at Heather's performance on these specific subtests plays a role in the diagnosis of whether ADHD rests on the sea floor for her (see Chapter 7).

Comparing IQ Scores with Previous Testing

Once I have the current VIQ and FIQ scores, I compare them with any other assessments the youngster has had in the past (by me or another clinician). Even though the popular notion is that IQ is a quantifiable and unchanging score – in reality there are many factors which affect it, causing such to go up or down over time. Hence, differences in *Paper IQ* for a maltreated child over the years is a virtual given. However, the typical pattern is to see neglected or abused kiddoes' *Paper FIQ* gradually increase, the longer they live in a stable home environment.

Remember the old saying that there are few absolutes in this world? Well, there is at least **one** absolute that I can think of in *my* field. A maltreated child will always score out lower on an IQ test than his genetic potential, **years** into a stable/loving home. How do I know this? Because I have had the opportunity to serially test boatloads of such young persons – the same kids over and over – up through late adolescence.

> ...the popular notion is that IQ is a quantifiable and unchanging score – in reality there are many factors which affect it causing such to go up or down over time.

I will perhaps first see a psychologically hurt child at age 5, then again at 8, then again at 12, then 15, and a last time at 17 or 18 – perhaps five times throughout the years – the same youngster. I now have a sizable number of this kind of serial assessment. As stated above, there almost always is a gradual increase in measured *Paper IQ* – as these young persons become stabilized in a good home, *and* are provided with a sound treatment plan along the way.

Calculating Genetic Verbal IQ

Oftentimes maltreated youth have to reach age 19 to 22 *before they are able to demonstrate their God-given potential on an IQ test*. Fortunately though, we can use individual neuropsychologic subtests to project what their constitutional verbal intelligence actually *is*, well before, say, age 21.

However, on occasion a **diminution** in *Paper VIQ* occurs. This regression is generally due to one of three reasons: (1) either the youngster is providing a less than stellar effort during current testing (despite our best efforts to elicit thorough participation); (2) there is a runaway stagecoach ADHD; or (3) there has been an exacerbation in overall emotionality since the previous testing. In the latter, such possibilities include: onset of a Borderline Condition, Schizophrenia, and/or a Childhood Bipolar Disorder. Or perhaps an environmental change has occurred such as a recent termination of parental rights, a change in placement only 2 months ago, etc.

In addition, there are indicators on *other* various tests I use which can indicate whether any recent depression/anxiety – due to genetic or stress-related factors – may be producing a regression of the *Paper VIQ* (see Chapter 11).

Moreover, another reason for a downward spiral in functional IQ might be caused by a recent traumatic brain injury (see Chapter 4), or a functional/neurologic learning disability (see Chapter 6) which is not being addressed.

Parents, Take Heart!

It can be very disheartening to parents if they get back a *Paper VIQ* score of 74 on their child. They think, "Gosh, a 74. This is *bad*. My child is not very bright. And, she is *never* going to be very bright."

Fortunately, as stated above, there are many additional factors we look for in the neuropsychologic profile that give us a sneak-preview of the estimated God-given genetic VIQ of your child – regardless of what the current *Paper VIQ* might be.

In the example above, let's say Heather tests out to a WISC-III *Paper VIQ* of 74. However, her WISC-III Similarities subtest scores out to an IQ-equivalent of 105. Moreover, on WISC-III Vocabulary, she rings in at a 110. In that instance, an averaging (or mean) of the two comes to a 107.5 – or a 108 (rounded up). Thus, despite Heather's *Paper VIQ* of 74, *her estimated God-given genetic verbal intelligence is more consistent with approximately a 108,* as opposed to what we glean from the present WISC-III *Paper VIQ or FIQ*. This is a 34 point difference! Not uncommon to see, among youth with histories of maltreatment.

> Fortunately…there are many additional factors we look for in the neuropsychologic profile that can give us a sneak-preview of the estimated God-given genetic VIQ of your child…

Summary

The Intelligence Quotient (IQ) of a youth can give us a partial snapshot as to the biologic/cortical functioning of the brain. Great care must be taken in interpreting IQ scores, however, inasmuch there are many variables which might skew the actual interpretation. Nevertheless, being cognizant of both the current *Paper IQ* **as well as** generic/God-given intelligence helps us know what we can expect out of a youngster – now and in the future – an important factor in our undersea exploration.

Chapter 6

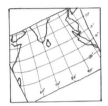

Checking Coordinates: Neurologic and Functional Learning Disabilities

There is an important distinction to make between Learning Disabilities (LD): *neurologic* and *functional*. A neurologic LD is due to a physiologic anomaly in the brain. The hard-wiring is somehow slightly askew, typically either a congenital condition – the result of in utero drug/alcohol abuse – or due to genetics. Traumatic brain injuries can also produce a neurologic LD.

A functional Learning Disability, on the other hand, while sharing many of the same outward appearances as a neurologic LD (i.e., Mark cannot read, do simple long division, etc), is due to a very different cause. Part of the reality for us who use psychologic and neuropsychologic reports is that we cannot take everything at face value. I cannot take all the numbers I get from test data without marrying them to the youth's history, past circumstances, as well as an understanding of the subtleties for each test.

Navigating the Currents

However, determining whether a Learning Disability is neurologic or functional is not something I acquired in graduate school, I am sorry to say. I have ascertained it via the proverbial *School of Hard Knocks* – following children, testing them, retesting them, then retesting them again – learning, through experience, what these various measures reveal.

It is possible that when a young person comes into my clinic for an evaluation, I see what on the surface *appears* to be a Learning Disability. The question becomes: "Is this a functional or neurologic LD?" As I explore Mark's background, I find he has had a deprived early childhood. The youngster has perhaps received a paucity of outside stimulation. He has been passed around among various relatives – as though he was an old sofa – and was severely neglected.

> ...determining whether a Learning Disability is neurologic or functional is not something I acquired in graduate school, I am sorry to say.

Social Services ultimately learns of the situation and visits the home. They say, "This is not a good thing. Let's take this youngster and put him with a stable family." And so it happens. Now, Mark starts Kindergarten. But remember, his exposure to the outside world has been very limited.

Will Mark *look* LD when he gets to school? Of course he will. Big time. This young student has the appearance of a severe Learning Disability. He doesn't know his colors. He doesn't know his numbers. He knows very little about anything.

However, does that mean that there is something actually wrong with his brain? Does that mean the left temporo-parietal lobe (one of the frequent *hot-spots* for neurologic brain-based Language Learning Disabilities) is flawed? Not necessarily. What *may* happen when this type of youngster is placed into a stable home is that he will begin to catch up. It might take him a year or two or three to come up to grade level, but often, over time, he does.

50

One thing I would like to point out is that some young children who have been underexposed to appropriate pre-academic enrichment can develop a *neurologic* LD due to a lack of opportunity for certain forms of brain hard-wiring to occur. For example, if Heather, has been left alone in a *closet* during ages, say, 2 to 3, she may have truly acquired a neurologic LD within the realm of expressive language. Due to the lack of input, a child's young brain may miss the normal stimulation required during the developmental window that, say, expressive language needs.

> Due to the lack of input, a child's young brain may miss the normal stimulation required during the developmental window that, say, expressive language needs.

Functional Learning Disability

At any rate, a functional Learning Disability will frequently appear in a youngster who has had a partially deprived early childhood. Mark has been read to only sporadically; he has not been allowed to explore his environment very much; nor has anyone been there to help him interpret the world on a consistent basis. Remember, Mark has been passed around from relative to relative. Plus – maybe because of multiple placements – he has, by age 10, already attended six different **schools**. Learning opportunities have been hit or miss (fairly good at school #s two and four, but poor at school #s one, three, five, and six).

But fortunately, as stated before, in time, a functional Learning Disability can often be overcome – much easier than is the case for a neurologic LD.

Neurologic Learning Disability

One example of a brain-based Learning Disability is Dyslexia – a 4th grader who still reverses letters, displays primitive spelling, and yields dysgraphic writing (much like an MD's signature on a prescription!). Or, a child might have a mathematics Learning Disability: Dyscalculia – a clinical term for problems in addition, subtraction, multiplication, etc. These LDs are a result of a dysfunction in the brain, not simply from a spotty tenure of school attendance during 3rd grade, etc.

> ...a functional Learning Disability will frequently appear in a youngster who has had a partially deprived early childhood.

As stated above, it needs to be emphasized, however, that as a result of the lack of stimulation during critical developmental *windows*, the child's brain *can be* deleteriously affected – bringing about a neurologic LD for a young person in whom no congenital brain anomalies otherwise exist.

So, in essence, for Learning Disabilities, drawing a distinction between a neurologic vs. a functional LD is needed – *because* there **is** a big difference between the outcomes, or prognosis, of the two types. Of course, we need to address the Learning Disability. However, *how* and to what extent we deal with it is going to be different – depending upon whether the lean academic skills are due to a neurologic *or* to a functional LD.

Woodcock-Johnson Revised

One of the assessment tools I use when I *scuba dive* to determine whether a child possesses a functional or neurologic Learning Disability is the Woodcock Johnson Revised (WJ-R).

The WJ-R gives me a detailed analysis of academic skills (and can sometimes *help* tell me how *bright* a kiddo really is, to boot). This test measures: reading, math, and writing skills (the *Three R's*). I then compare Mark's scores against actual grade placement. When a kiddo receives a low score on any academic achievement test, it is imperative to know how to interpret the results. For example, it is my job to determine whether a low phonics score is a sign of a phonetic Learning Disability *or* if such is simply the result of Heather having been immersed in a Whole Language Learning System year after year at school.

> The WJ-R gives me a detailed analysis of academic skills (and can sometimes *help* tell me how *bright* a kiddo really is, to boot).

This is why I gather as much information as possible about the child's background, school/educational history, etc – so I will have as many pieces necessary to complete the puzzle and arrive at a true diagnosis.

In general, weaknesses in WJ-R scores *can* point to a neurologic Learning Disability. It can also tell if a child is simply *at risk* for the eventual diagnosis of an LD. Moreover, the various indices can help reveal various organic compromises in the brain, as well.

> When a kiddo receives a low score on any academic achievement test, it is imperative to know how to interpret the results.

Additionally, the WJ-R can also provide evidence of a higher genetic intellect than what is reflected via a *Paper VIQ*. The Reading, Math, and Writing Clusters often serve as better estimates of God-given/biologic intellect than do scores off an actual IQ test such as the WISC-III, Kaufman, Stanford-Binet, etc. Any of the various WJ-R Clusters can be utilized, along with the child's highest two WISC-III Verbal Subtest scores – to obtain clues as to an estimated God-given VIQ.

Gray Writing Samples Test

Another tool I use to augment the WJ-R's language assessment is the Gray Writing Samples Test (Gray, 1994). We present two action pictures for the youth to write whatever he desires regarding the scenes. For young children, we dictate the 26 letters of the English alphabet to him (out of sequence) for the kiddo to write on a piece of paper. If he is unable to write the letters via *dictation*, we will then allow him to simply copy them one at a time. So, GWST are individually tailored to the age and writing skill competency of the youngster.

The GWST can reveal Graphic Dyspraxia (an impairment in the quality of printing/cursive), or Dyslexia (difficulties in general language – substituting "d"s for "b"s, improper usage of capital letters, spelling problems, incorrect verb usage, etc). Neurologic written Language LDs (sometimes referred to as Language Learning Disorders – LLDs) most commonly point to left tertiary integration dysfunction (the region in the left hemisphere where the frontal, temporal, and parietal lobes *join* one another).

> In assessing youngsters who have suffered histories of…(chaotic families, neglect, etc)…we must allow **them** to attain at least a mid 3rd grade status, or age 9½ – whichever occurs **last** – before a neurologic LD can accurately be diagnosed…

Determining Learning Disabilities

In assessing youngsters who have suffered histories of early narcissistic injuries (chaotic families, neglect, etc), in my experience, we must allow **them** to attain at least a mid 3rd grade status, or age 9½ – whichever occurs **last** – before a neurologic LD can accurately be diagnosed (except in extreme cases).

There are simply times when a child will be too young for us to accurately determine whether a brain-based LD exists or not. But, as stated, I have found mid 3rd grade or age 9½ to be the best cut-off. There have been a lot of psychologists over the years (the author included) who, for example, prematurely diagnosed a *young* child as neurologic LD – only to discover a mere year later, that he had caught up in school, and was academically functioning on grade level. I have a basement full of old ties with splattered egg on them.

Nonverbal Learning Disabilities

Nonverbal Learning Disabilities (NLD) is a neurologic condition most generally thought to emanate from the right cerebral hemisphere. Reception and processing of nonverbal stimuli are problematic (Rourke, 1995).

Youth with NLD are thought to frequently **struggle** with:
  ▷ motor coordination/balance
  ▷ visual-spatial skills
  ▷ social judgment – involving the discombobulation of social cues given off by others

Children with NLD are thought to have the following **strengths**:
  ▷ early speech and vocabulary development
  ▷ robust rote memory skills
  ▷ early development of reading/spelling
  ▷ verbal eloquence
  ▷ strong auditory retention

For me, NLD is a difficult syndrome to fully get my arms around – at least among maltreated young persons. For example, some experts within this domain indicate that strong attention to detail is usually typical for NLD kiddoes. Others disagree, stating that such youngsters **struggle** with attention/concentration. I think most agree however that NLD is rife with comorbid conditions.

Additionally, the **strengths** generally touted for NLD kiddoes (see above) are frequently absent within the majority of maltreated youth. That is, I rarely see neglected/abused youngsters demonstrate early speech/vocabulary development/reading/spelling/verbal eloquence.

Who knows what percentage of the maltreated youth I see would **otherwise have presented** with said NLD strengths (generally attributed to a robust left hemisphere, by the way) had they not been neglected or abused early on. As is known, mistreatment often closes down early childhood windows of language-based development. Thus, for clinicians working among populations of **non-maltreated** youth, instances of NLD are probably more prevalent than is the case for me.

Summary
Determining whether Mark or Heather has a functional or neurologic Learning Disability has implications for the prognosis of a child's academic success. With a neurologic LD, the prognosis is more guarded. With a functional LD, the prognosis is better. Either, however, will demand the same sort of tutorials. It's just that we must be more persistent and patient with kiddoes beset by a brain-based LD. With the neurologic LD child, remember, it's a marathon – not a sprint.

Chapter 7

Powerful Undertow:
Attention Deficit Hyperactivity Disorder

ADD or ADHD? Currently there is confusion over the mere *terms* ADD (Attention Deficit Disorder) and ADHD (Attention Deficit Hyperactivity Disorder). The names do not reflect two different genres of attention deficit, but rather merely different **editions** of the DSM (Diagnostic and Statistical Manual of Mental Disorders – the official *Bible* of the mental health field). The current nomenclature is Attention Deficit Hyperactivity Disorder. So even a child who struggles with auditory/visual attention, but is not hyperactive, is said to possess this syndrome (without hyperactivity). I wish we had simply kept the old DSM-III-R nomenclature of ADD with hyperactivity, and ADD without hyperactivity. Often, simpler is better. However, at times, common horse sense eludes those of us in the mental health field.

Brain Structure

You will remember from our discussion of the brain that the human pre-frontal lobes are right behind the forehead – as I have said, the CEO of a corporation, if you will. They oversee most everything that happens within the brain. In simplistic fashion, the theory of ADHD is that there is some sort of neurochemical imbalance, subtle as it may be, that is causing a portion of pre-frontal lobe neurons to misfire.

> ...the human pre-frontal lobes are right behind the forehead...the CEO of a corporation, if you will.

Such results in the characteristic hyperactivity, impulsivity, lack of concentration, and/or inattention of a child. Some of these behaviors (e.g., the hyperactivity) seem to be a reaction on the part of Mark for purposes of non-consciously self-stimulating the pre-frontal portions of his brain. Once the neurochemical imbalance is addressed through medication, many maladaptive behaviors improve, or disappear (for as long as the medication is in Mark's system).

The impact of pre-frontal lobe compromise is easy to see in persons who have suffered trauma to that area. For example, folks who have sustained head injuries, and I have seen a lot of them as a neuropsychologist, will often struggle to regain these neuropathways. I remember one adult male I was working with who had been in a car accident. In the crash he had hit his head on the windshield and remained unconscious for approximately 48 hours. I talked to him about 6 months post-accident.

> Once the neurochemical imbalance is addressed through medication, many maladaptive behaviors improve, or disappear...

"Jim, how are you doing?"

"Well, you know, I'm doing *pretty* well. I'm able to perform most of the things I could do before the accident. My memory finally seems to be back. The headaches are *way* fewer. I no longer get so confused at work, and I'm up to almost half-time there. Doing much better. Except for one thing."

"What's that, Jim?"

"Well, it's the strangest thing. I *cannot* watch a 30-minute TV program anymore. My favorite sitcom is *Coach* – you know, the one with Hayden Fox as coach of the Minnesota State Screaming Eagles. I can only sit through about 15 minutes of it until I just have to get up. It's too much for me. I just have stop watching!

"And the same thing with a movie. I can make it through – *maybe* – a half hour, and then I have to get up and walk around. It's just too much of a drain on me – on my brain, I guess. It almost *hurts* to sit there and try to watch it, after about 30 minutes..."

Basically, Jim's pre-frontal lobes had not yet fully recovered from the car crash and resultant head trauma. One of the important functions of this brain region is to help us with attention and concentration. When Jim tried to watch his favorite TV program or a movie, he had big-time difficulty concentrating. Fully functioning pre-frontal lobes screen out extraneous stimuli, whether visual or auditory. Jim's were not able to do this just yet; therefore, he had trouble concentrating on specific jobs. Fortunately, after another 6 months, his brain compensated, and his ability to pay attention and concentrate *healed*.

> Fully functioning pre-frontal lobes screen out extraneous stimuli, whether visual or auditory.

For example, if you are at home with your family, and all the chatter around were to suddenly cease, you would most likely say it is quiet. But really, if you truly listen, many noises persist: the whine of the air conditioner, faint traffic sounds from a nearby street, perhaps even a bird's melody outside the window. Your pre-frontal lobes have screened out *these* distractions, enabling you to read or focus in on what someone is saying, etc. Our pre-frontal lobes are great screeners.

For ADHD youngsters, it is as if their *screeners* have shut down. The child becomes distractible. His concentration wanes. He gets side-tracked. For **these** kiddoes, the problem is that their pre-frontal lobes have not yet *matured* to the point that they can filter out distracting stimuli. Many ADHD youth simply become overly bombarded with auditory and/or visual stimuli. This is one of the reasons that the old worn-out fad of *open classrooms* proved such a bust.

Lifespan of ADHD

Fortunately, I find that many youth *outgrow* their ADHD as their pre-frontal lobes mature naturally. Such is in direct contradistinction to a minority of professionals in the field who chant the mantra: "ADHD – you are *born* with it, and you will *die* with it."

Such has clearly not been **my** experience. Rather, in the longitudinal case studies I have seen, the percentages appear to be, as below.

ADHD Progression Rates

> 80% of ADHD youth outgrowing the disorder by their mid-teen years (age 15ish)

> 10% of ADHD youth outgrowing the disorder by their mid-collegiate years
> (age 20ish)

> 10% of ADHD youth *not* outgrowing the disorder, carrying such across the
> lifespan (those who are dubbed "Adult ADHD")

Figure 7.1   ADHD Progression Rates

So, for 90% of youngsters diagnosed with a bona fide ADHD, the odds are on their side that they will likely mature *out of* the syndrome, given enough time for their pre-frontal lobes to develop. The percentages in Figure 7.1 above are derived from my own experience, swimming beneath the oceans' channels, year after year. They are not based on research.

Testing for ADHD

You will often hear it said, "There *is* no test for ADHD." True and not true. While there is no **one** measure capable of diagnosing this syndrome, if a *battery* of attention-sensitive procedures is used, we can pinpoint the disorder quite well – via an ADHD Weighting Scale. From years of working with kiddoes, and making careful observations, I stumbled upon such. Said scale uses a *cluster* of tests. Taken together, this concoction can depict whether or not ADHD is part of the muck I find for Mark during my scuba expedition on his behalf. See Figure 7.2 for a rundown on the specific attention-sensitive measures **I** use.

Each of the individual ADHD-sensitive test results is placed on the Attention Deficit Hyperactivity Weighting Scale (Gray, 1996). The results provide a quantifiable profile of attention/concentration behaviors, from which a very good picture of a youth's ADHD status can be deduced. As I stated earlier, we cannot hang our hat on any *single* test for this syndrome.

> While there is no **one** measure capable of diagnosing this syndrome, if a *battery* of attention-sensitive procedures is used, we can pinpoint the disorder quite well...

Some of the behaviors typically associated with ADHD can actually stem from a *variety* of sources, such as depression or anxiety (see Chapter 11), a Choleric temperament (see Chapter 8) – as well as others. But if we just rear back and call the youngster ADHD – based solely on his *overt actions*, or from a simplistic check-list – as was especially prevalent back in the 80s, we do the kiddo a real disservice.

Many of these non-ADHD children were diagnosed as such and placed on Ritalin. One of two things happened: (1) either *nothing* occurred; they might as well have been given inert sugar pills; or (2) they had adverse side-effects.

Moreover, I cannot **tell** you how many youth I have seen who have had all kinds of behavioral syndromes going on below the waterline – *including* ADHD – wherein the

> ...I cannot **tell** you how many youth I have seen who have had all kinds of behavioral syndromes going on below the waterline – *including* ADHD – wherein the only disorder on the **tip** of the iceberg *was* ADHD.

only disorder on the **tip** of the iceberg *was* ADHD. The true sea-bearing refuse from the bottom of the gulf all too often consisted of other entities: perhaps a Borderline Condition (see Chapter 9), Bipolar Disorder (see Chapter 10), and so on – in some cases sharing the ocean floor *with* this syndrome – in many other instances *not*.

Thus, in order to best help Mark, I need to know the source of the problem. If the underlying root cause is actually a masked depression, treating him for ADHD will not help. The specific attention-sensitive tests mentioned above assist in fleshing out the causal agent of his rotten behaviors.

Mark's ADHD

The parameters of the Attention Deficit Hyperactivity Weighting Scale **I** use are tabled below. There appears to be a 2-point error vari-

Attention Deficit Hyperactivity Weighting Scale

(Mark's Sample)*

Modality	Weighting	Modality	Weighting
TESTING SESSION		**GORDON**	
Fidgets/Impulsive	1	Delay	
Motoric Over-Activity		Vigilance	
Poor Attention	2	Distractibility	1
SCHOOL SETTING		Commission Errors	
Fidgets/Impulsive	2	**TAD**	
Motoric Over-Activity		Quiet	
Poor Attention	2	Distractibility	2
PIC		**STROOP**	
ADHD		Word	1
LITTAUER		Color	
Primary Sanguine	3	Color-Word	
Secondary Sanguine		**SPEECH SOUNDS**	
WISC-III		Distractibility	
Arithmetic		**SEASHORE RHYTHM**	
Digit Span	1	Distractibility	2
Coding	1	**REITAN-KLOVE TACTILE**	
Picture Completion	1	Distractibility	1
		Distractibility	1
		TOTAL	**21**

* Numbers above reveal ADHD–specific tests which Mark had difficulty with. If there is a blank, such indicates Mark *aced* that particular ADHD-sensitive test.

ADHD Weighting Scale Totals

Raw Score				Range
0	—	12	=	WNL
13	—	16	=	Mild Range
17	—	20	=	Moderate Range
21	—	↑	=	Severe Range
Scores > 13 are positive for ADHD				

Figure 7.2 Attention Deficit Hyperactivity Weighting Scale

ance with it. This means that if a child scores out at 21 on this measure, *Truth* with a Capital "T," in terms of that youngster's ADHD severity, can be anywhere from a 19 to a 23.

In the sample above, it can be seen that Mark gauges out to a raw score of 21 on the ADHD Weighting Scale. Such rests within the Severe range. And, this is while on his current regimen of Adderall 10 mg bid (twice a day). As such, Mark's ADHD Weighting Scale tells us what, about the effectiveness of his Adderall? That it's not doing the job. Mark may need his dosage increased. Or, he may need to be switched to *another* psychostimulant. Either will be per the discretion of Mark's personal physician.

Medication During Testing

As I mentioned in Chapter 2, if Mark is currently on psychotropics for ADHD, it is important that he take such, as normally scheduled, on the day of testing. The results of the evaluation can help me judge the efficacy of this medication. Thus, if the child has a pronounced ADHD raw score, even *with* his meds that day, the exam generally indicates the dosage needs to be increased, *or* that he might fare better on a *different* medication.

In similar fashion, if an ADHD youth is *already* taking a psychotropic for this condition and his scores are WNL (within normal limits) on the Weighting Scale, it generally indicates the meds are *working*. If the measure's raw score is *really* low, say a 6 or 7, then it might behoove us to decrease the psychotropic, on a trial basis, to see if the youngster has outgrown this disorder (usually due to pre-frontal lobe maturation).

On the other hand, if parents are unsure whether their kiddo truly *has* ADHD – despite the fact that someone assigned the diagnosis 4 years ago – and placed him on, say, Adderall – in *this* instance, we will elect to test the youngster *off* his Adderall, to see how he does. If the youth tests out WNL on the ADHD Weighting Scale, either one of two situations exist: (1) he has matured out of the disorder; or (2) the child never really *had* ADHD in the first place, having been misdiagnosed 4 years ago.

Summary

An ADHD diagnosis requires careful work, sifting through the various tests which are sensitive to attention/concentration, as well as taking into account what, if any, medications the child is on. Misdiagnosing a youngster, who, for example, is actually *depressed* as opposed to ADHD, does not help him. To be of any service, we must paint on the *large* canvas – i.e., figuring out first of all if this syndrome exists or not – and then second, what *other* comorbid (coexisting) underwater gunk is also present. If the diagnosis **is** ADHD, there is much that can be done for the child. Treatment options are discussed in Chapters 14, 15, 16, and 19.

Classroom Considerations for the ADHD Child
Adapted from Dr. Keith Conners (1999)

- Teacher should be knowledgeable and believe in the validity of ADHD as a syndrome
- Child has own seat (no tables with two to three other youngsters at it, etc)
- Seat is near front of classroom (to restrict visual distractions)
- No *open* classrooms
- Clear listing of the rules
- Occasional *review* of the rules
- Have the child repeat back rules/directions on occasion
- *Moderate* level of visual stimuli in the room
- Predictable routine
- Minimal unstructured time
- In assigning classwork and homework, teacher gives in manageable *bite-size* pieces:
  - (a) break up long assignments into smaller units with shorter dead lines
  - (b) follow the Premack Principle (*Grandma's Law*): follow a less desirable task with an enjoyable task
- Provide opportunities for motor movement (occasionally allowing child to wipe the board, sharpen pencils, etc)
- Utilize classroom computers – the highly interactive, multi-sensory nature of computer software is very effective in reducing a child's distractibility
- Multi-sensory directions (e.g., holding up a sign that says "Time to Stop" while saying "Time to Stop")
- Use of calm/soothing voice
- Token system (used similar to money so as to earn privileges/items, etc)
- The use of professionals/volunteers to aid in behavioral management
- Train motivated teachers to train *other* teachers, vis-à-vis ADHD children

Chapter 8

Underwater Terrain: Psychologic Temperament

Human psychologic temperament is thought to be chiefly derived from God-given genetics, plus the first 6 years of life experiences. Most experts on the topic classify people according to 4 basic personality groupings. Much of the following material is taken from the work of Tim LaHaye, along with Florence and Fred Littauer. All are Christian speakers and writers who have done many seminars and written profusely within this area (LaHaye, 1993; Littauer, 1992). Another notable Christian author/speaker of our day (Smalley, 1990) uses the same temperament groupings as does LaHaye and the Littauers; he simply employs different names (discussed below).

The four temperaments are: Choleric, Sanguine, Phlegmatic, and Melancholic. I use a test called the *Personality Profile*, consisting of 40 fill-in-the blank choices, developed by the Littauers (Littauer, 1983). This instrument helps identify a child's primary and secondary temperaments, and is typically completed by the young person's parent/adult caretaker.

Choleric

The first personality style is known as the Choleric/Lion. (*Choleric* is LaHaye/Littauer-speak; *Lion* is from Smalley). This particular temperament is an extrovert who thrives on taking charge of the situation at hand. You will find many a Choleric as CEOs of organizations and businesses. Folks with this temperament are *natural born leaders* – determined and self-sufficient. They are immensely goal-oriented, not infrequently a classic *Type A* personality.

Because the Choleric *is so driven*, she can get into trouble by demanding too much from others. She can also impress as bossy, opinionated, and short-tempered.

A youngster possessing the Choleric bent is generally viewed as the most difficult temperament of kiddo to rear, quite the challenge to parents. These youth typically display stubbornness and oppositionalism – the classic *strong-willed* child, to use Dr. James Dobson's terminology (Dobson, 1978). Our mission as parents is to help these youth successfully navigate their formative years, short of causing tachycardia (rapid heart rate) in ourselves.

> A youngster possessing the Choleric bent is generally viewed as the most difficult temperament of kiddo to rear, quite the challenge to parents.

Sanguine

You can easily recognize the Sanguine/Otter in a group setting – he is the person affectionately known as *the life of the party* (an obvious extrovert). A Sanguine loves to talk and visit. He lives life enthusiastically, is optimistic, full of energy. Young male Sanguines are frequently dubbed by teachers as *Class Clowns*.

And, of course, while he is busy having so much fun, the rest of his life becomes undisciplined, messy, with nothing ever finished! Other weaknesses include inconsistency, disorganization with school-work, and absent-mindedness.

As a general rule, a young Sanguine will struggle mightily with boring/run-of-the-mill activities. Additionally, he regularly takes the Olympic Gold for organizational problems, along with poor planning and lax impulse control. Thus, these young persons often place too little emphasis on studying for school tests, getting projects ready, etc. There are almost invariably *MIA* homework papers during the academic years (shot down somewhere over Laos or Cambodia), unless external structure – by adults – is provided.

> Young male Sanguines are frequently dubbed by teachers as *Class Clowns*.

I recall a few years back there was a Sanguine psychologist/author who had agreed to do a parent seminar at a local church in my city. Everyone was excited; a good crowd had assembled; refreshments were primed (cookies, corn chips, the ever-present Rotel dip, along with cherry punch – remember, I'm a Baptist – one cannot *have* a Baptist social function of any sort, sans these ingredients).

Anyway, it came time for the speaker to arrive. 15 minutes passed. Then 30. Then 45. Finally, someone from our group called the psychologist's home phone number (it was a Saturday). He answered, sheepishly admitting he had merely *forgotten*. An honest man! The speaker confessed he had been having fun with his family that day and time had merely gotten away from him! Classic Sanguine…

The individual also, by his own admission, suffered from adult ADHD. Anyway, the seminar was rescheduled. Dutiful Baptist that I was/am, I reluctantly agreed to, uh, reacquisition the assembled victuals. Thus, the apt moniker of *The Amazing El Consumo* for me was born (although my wife and teen-age son swear such was clearly a pre-morbid condition).

Phlegmatic

The Phlegmatic/Golden Retriever is kindly and introverted. This person makes a great compadre, inasmuch as she is able to get along with most everybody, is friendly, a good listener, and very loyal. She is frequently – outwardly at least – pleasant and patient. The Phlegmatic is cooperative – the notoriously easiest temperament of child to raise.

> The Phlegmatic is cooperative –
> the notoriously
> easiest temperament
> of child to raise.

On the other hand, like all the other personality types, there are weak- nesses. Frequent adjectives for the Phlegmatic consist of: timid, worrisome, fearful, and indecisive. This individual would rather bite a pig than enter into conflict with someone. The same goes for change. She also can have a tendency to keep emotions close to the vest. Anger is a four-letter word. Phlegmatics are typically very uncomfortable with expressing hostility. In fact, many are not even aware when they *experience* anger!

Melancholic

The Melancholic/Beaver, the second of the two introverted temperaments, is the consummate perfectionist – detailed, task-oriented, orderly, analytical, organized. This person is able to see what needs to be done, and accomplish it – a real worker bee.

As the name suggests, however,

> The Melancholic...
> is the consummate
> perfectionist –
> detailed, task-
> oriented, orderly,
> analytical, organized.

Melancholics *can* be prone toward depression/anxiety off and on throughout his life. Other weaknesses of this introverted temperament are hypersensitivity, moodiness, and compulsivity. He can also come across at times to others as insecure and difficult to please. A Melancholic may also be perceived as something of a *loner*.

Understanding One Another

Generally, people are identified by two of the four temperaments. For instance, Mark might be Sanguine/Phlegmatic, or Choleric/Sanguine. Just to let you know a little about myself, I test out as a primary Choleric/secondary Melancholic. So, I possess both extroverted as well as introverted tendencies. And, this admixture is not uncommon among people.

I am the kind of person who likes to *get on the horse and ride*. I tend to make decisions reasonably quickly, but my Melancholic side says that before I *make* a choice, I need to get *all* the information – *all* the data. I want to have my ducks in a row – "*t*"s crossed, and "*i*"s dotted. Such a penchant for detail, as any law abiding Sanguine will attest, drives them absolutely berserk.

"A plan, a blueprint?! Hey, let's just **ride**. Let it **eat**!" Any self-respecting Sanguine would say: "Just *do* it!"

For almost 7 years my family had the pleasure of membership at Lake Arlington Baptist Church in Arlington, Texas – in the heart of the Dallas/Fort Worth metroplex. Our pastor – my friend and golf buddy – is Dr. David George, who has been with the church for over 30 years. Dr. G, the consummate Sanguine/Choleric, tended to pursue vacation-time in this fashion: "Hey, let's get in the car and start driving…What? Where are we going? **I** don't know…Motel reservations? Uh, no. Why don't we just head to Colorado…" Again, classic Sanguine.

Anyway, as I was saying, I am a Choleric/Melancholic. My wife, on the other hand, is a decided Melancholic/Phlegmatic. (Please never let her know that I am writing this. Thanks.) Hence, *she* scores out very high on the introverted side of the coin. She also is a meticulous person. Debbi likes her life very ordered. Change is unacceptable. Her Phlegmatic/Golden Retriever side renders her kindly, *and* much more patient than I. She is a wonderful listener and has, at last count, at least 23 best friends. Said another way, she is best friend to 23 different people. How do I know this, you ask? It is because these 23 individuals call our house constantly. Years ago we bought an answering machine so as to preserve our marriage. But, I digress.

When talking to a lady friend, Debbi might, for example, ask her about something mentioned 3 or 4 months ago. The typical reply is, "I can't even remember *telling you* that; you must *really listen.*"

> My belief is God *chisels us* and helps mature us, via our spouse.

And she does. Over the course of our 22+ year marriage, we have gleaned from each other – taken on some of the characteristics each of us possess. My belief is God *chisels us* and helps mature us, via our spouse. Debbi is now more assertive; I am more patient. However, I still do not have 23 best friends; nor do people call me on the telephone. But, I'm not bitter about this at all…

So, What's the *Fuss*?!

Well, the big deal with temperament is that it is important to know the basic bedrock personality style of our kids. For example, if my child is an oppositional little twit more often than not, how much of it is due to his Cholericism? If his outbursts are due to his temperament, we are going to need much different disciplinary forays with him, than if he is merely a Melancholic youth within the throes of a masked depression, for instance.

Understanding temperaments also helps us more effectively *train up* our children in the way they should go (Proverbs 22:6). Debbi's

72

mother and late father would tell you that on the 3 occasions growing up wherein she got in trouble for something (between birth and high school graduation), all they ever had to do for discipline was....*look* at her. ***Look*** at her! That was *it*. Prior to my parents going to be with the Lord, back in the Spring of '98, I tried mightily to keep my in-laws, Bob and Maxine, from comparing notes with Ed and Juanita. Because I was a classic little Choleric/strong-willed brat – sort of an oppositional Dennis the Menace *gone south*.

For fun sometime, try *merely looking at* a child of this ilk – *caught* in the midst of transgressing. See what happens...Right. He will laugh, spit, curse, fume, throw, and/or hit. Bottom line, a youngster's temperament will help guide us to the most appropriate means of discipline.

When we write parenting books that say **one** *size fits all* in terms of discipline, we are talking psychosis-on-parade.

I always get a kick out of professionals – usually well-meaning – who write parenting books, without taking into account a child's particular temperament. Generally, the message is: "If you just read my book, you will be able to handle any youngster living under your roof. Just follow my boiler-plate checklist of procedures."

When we write parenting books that say ***one*** *size fits all* in terms of discipline, we are talking psychosis-on-parade. That is about as kind as I can say it. It takes **many** different approaches to effectively deal with our children – and their varied temperament combinations. (By the way, if you will just read *this* book, then never again will your kiddo...)

Parental Temperaments

As parents, it is also very helpful to understand our *own* temperament. I mentioned earlier, I am a Choleric/Melancholic (the latter being perfectionist and meticulous). Recall that my wife also possesses Melancholic, along with Phlegmatic. Hence, the two of us have to be careful to let our son be who *he* is – not expecting him to be like either of *us*. This is a risk factor for Melancholic parents – that their child will be expected to grow up as little miniature *thems*, always striving for perfection/meticulousness.

The same, of course, can be said of Sanguine parents (or any of the other temperaments). For example, this fun-loving, playful, spontaneous individual may not realize the need his Melancholic child has to be forewarned of changes in routine. Sanguines never tire of people, but the Melancholic youngster needs time by himself to recharge.

> Sanguines never tire of people, but the Melancholic youngster needs time by himself to recharge.

Keeping in mind the differences between our own temperament, as parents, and that of our children, we can prevent undue strain on family relationships. Furthermore, it helps prevent *us* from expecting our youth to conform to who *we* are. Whatever our personality style, we cannot live our own lives vicariously via our offspring – be they biologic, foster, or adoptive.

Temperaments: Clinical Lore

Children having behavioral difficulties, or those in the foster care system, are often evaluated every few years to update their treatment plans. Occasionally, a youngster will test out to a somewhat different Littauer profile from a previous assessment. Several factors can contribute to this phenomenon: (1) the youngster has *matured into* her true innate personality type; (2) acute stress factors have occurred since the prior evaluation; (3) sampling error (perhaps the profiles are filled out by different caregivers, in the case of foster youth, who may be moved from home to home every few years); and/or (4) psychologic *masking* (a child was perhaps within the *Honeymoon Stage* the first time a Littauer was completed on him – now that he is out of the *Honeymoon Stage*, his behavior is quite different).

One further note I need to make regarding temperaments is that there are two *unnatural* combinations, according to the Littauers: the Sanguine/Melancholic, and the Choleric/Phlegmatic. It is intuitively obvious that the Sanguine/Melancholic make for strange bedfellows, given the gregarious nature of the one – in contrast to the quiet/introspective quality of the other. Correspondingly, the Choleric's high drive, strong-willed decisiveness stands in contrast to the Phlegmatic's low-key, easygoing, more laid-back manner.

If a child is identified with one of these combinations, I need to investigate/rule out any of the following: (1) an identity disturbance; (2) a conscious or unconscious personality *masking*; and/or (3) a Borderline Condition (see Chapter 9).

Summary

Each of the temperaments has strengths and weaknesses. When parents understand the personality style of their youth, they are better able to discipline that child. Caregivers can then tailor their behavioral interventions to their own unique youngster. And by understanding our *own* temperament as parents, we can thus be aware of the danger of imposing *our* personality onto a kiddo. This awareness helps us raise our children better. Remember, one size *doesn't* fit all, when it comes to discipline – or to most anything **else** in life, for that matter.

Chapter 9

Choppy Waters: Borderline Conditions of Childhood/Adolescence

This syndrome is perhaps the least understood of all undersea debris which can impact a troubled child. What I am referring to as Borderline Conditions among youth has its origin with Mahler, et al (1949), more recently documented via the work of Vela and Petti (1990) in what they term *Borderline Children* or *Borderline Disorders of Childhood*. Vela and Petti's model describes youth who present with some or all of the following: (1) difficulty relating to others; (2) acute anxiety; (3) impulsivity; (4) thought disturbance; (5) transient psychotic symptoms; and/or (6) delayed development.

Actually, Borderline Conditions (BCs) really should be broken into two camps: (1) the less severe variant – Borderline Syndrome of Childhood (BSC); and (2) the more extreme – Borderline Psychosis of Childhood (BPC). Parenthetically, when I refer to BSC or BPC, such applies to adolescents as well.

I also need to make clear that BCs is a wholly separate and distinct entity from Borderline Personality Disorder (see Chapter 12).

In essence, Borderline Conditions (BSC and BPC) are mental/emotional syndromes which rest within the *No Man's Land* between normalcy and florid psychosis. Although BCs are not actual entities within the DSM-IV (*Diagnostic and Statistical Manual-4th Edition*) – basically the mental health compendium – such does not alter my opinion of the validity of this syndrome.

The Borderline Conditions Continuum

The first question we need to answer is what does the term *psychosis* refer to? Such is merely a fancy way of saying, "I have done broke off from reality" (to quote some of my more rural friends). Psychotic folk do not see the world as the rest of us do. Basically, they have lost touch with what is real. These persons may be experiencing hallucinations – that is, hearing voices that are not there, seeing imaginary bats flying about the room, etc.

Delusions may also be present. Examples would be believing others are trying to covertly poison them, fearing the FBI is pursuing them, or perceiving that aliens are harassing them from the planet Zenon. Actually, *Childhood* Psychosis is very rare, just as Childhood Schizophrenia is very rare. (Schizophrenia is simply one of several forms of psychosis.)

Let us think about a continuum (see Figure 9.1). On the left side is what we can term *Buck Normal*. On the far left would be someone such as the late Mother Teresa, or Billy Graham, or perhaps a Dr. Brooks Taylor (a benevolent medical missionary to South America for many years, who grew up two doors down from me on Forrest Avenue in my hometown of Cleburne, Texas). The rest of us would fall in somewhere *close* to *buck normal*, albeit a tad more to the right of Mother Teresa, Billy Graham, and Brooks Taylor.

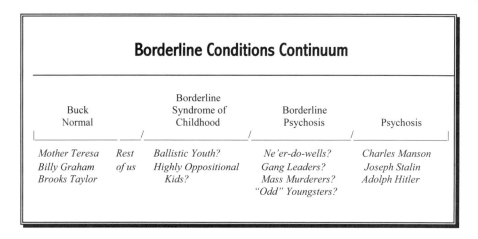

Figure 9.1   Borderline Conditions (BCs) Continuum

On the far right of the continuum we would have psychotic individuals. And not merely psychotic – actually psychotic *sociopaths*. People like Charles Manson, for instance. In fact, I see Chuck as the poster-boy for the Mother Teresa antithesis, if you will. The 2002 snipers, who terrified citizens of Washington D.C., are an example of either BP, **or** pure psychosis. But an Adolph Hitler or Joseph Stalin would be right there with Manson – in essence the quintessential psychotic sociopath: psychotic, in the sense that each has *broken off from reality*; sociopathic, in the sense that there is no *conscience* for these individuals.

That, after all, is the true *calling-card* of the sociopath – someone who lacks a *conscience*. And, it is my belief that some sociopaths learn their behavior from having been raised by other sociopaths. The rest of these delinquent individuals, in my view, are *born* lacking a *conscience*. Why do I say this? Because a significant percentage of them come from good parents and good families. But again, I digress.

Youngsters with Borderline Conditions, in my experience, are characterized by any or all of the following: (1) a mild perceptual distortion; (2) a subtle thought disorder; and/or (3) deviant fantasy operations. BPC can present with any **one**, any **two**, or all **three** of these characteristics. Again, when differentiating BSC from BPC, we are merely talking *degree* of the above three criteria.

When I do an evaluation, one of the things I always examine is where a youth lines up on the above BCs continuum. Fortunately, most children are either on the left side (normal), or in the middle somewhere (a BC). I only rarely see a youngster who is floridly psychotic (far right side of the continuum). If he is, the kiddo would most likely be in an RTC or psychiatric hospital. He would not be an outpatient.

Mild Perceptual Distortion

Let me more clearly describe what I mean by the term *mild perceptual distortion* (MPD). Remember, such can encompass either a Borderline Syndrome of Childhood (BSC), or Borderline Psychosis of Childhood (BPC). Many times youngsters with a BC misinterpret the cues and intentions that people, such as parents and teachers, direct toward them. This is what I was referring to above as a gunked-up filter. The perceptions they have of persons and situations around them differ from what you or I experience.

> Many times youngsters with a BC misinterpret the cues and intentions that people, such as parents and teachers, direct toward them.

For instance, an educator may calmly reprimand Heather at school, only to have the youngster go home that day and tell mom that said teacher really came down on her, yelled and humiliated her in front of all the other classmates, etc. However, in actuality an impartial observer of the situation would say, "Mrs. Jones just told her to turn back around, stop talking to Amanda, and get back to work – being respectful and low-key in her voice tone." Regardless, a kiddo with a BC is at times unable to *hear* the correction for what it really is.

Subtle Thought Disorder

A second potential *calling-card* of the BC is a *subtle thought disorder* (STD). Simply put, an STD is a mild *disconnect* within the thinking patterns of youth. For instance, one way we can see this is among youngsters who do a great deal of verbal **rambling**. Another example can be a kiddo who is what we call *tangential* – jumping from

> Simply put, an STD is a mild *disconnect* within the thinking patterns of youth.

unrelated topic to unrelated topic – making it very difficult for the listener to follow what the child or teen is trying to say.

As mentioned above, the thoughts (which *come out* of the young person as verbiage) just aren't woven together very tightly. If you frequently notice this in your child, chances are strong, he has just entered *The Twilight Zone* of STD. Pay attention to this.

Deviant Fantasy Operations

The term *deviant fantasy operations* (DFOs) is merely *shrink-speak* for deviant fantasy life. Whenever I listen to parents say that their youngster is *always coming up with wild-hare stories*, my little antennae go up in terms of wondering if DFOs are occurring. Almost always, in such instances, they are. And, these far-fetched stories can vary wildly.

On the least malignant end of the DFOs continuum might be a pre-adolescent boy – in actuality a chronic bench-warmer on the basketball team – who proclaims to one and all that he is the squad's *leading scorer*. A more pathologic rendition however is the teen-age girl who insists that an infant is ceremonially sacrificed by a group of

Satan worshippers in the woods behind her adoptive home every Saturday night.

Furthermore regarding the DFOs dynamic, it has been my experience that in almost every case, there is a **kernel** of truth to the particular wild-hare story. In the pre-adolescent male mentioned above, he **is** on the middle school basketball team – he simply however never plays. In the teenage girl scenario above, on most Saturday nights six or seven gang members in the forest behind her house physically *beat-up* a younger initiate (the new member's rite of passage to the ne'er-do-well group). But no one is killing any babies back there.

> Whenever I listen to parents say that their youngster is *always coming up with wild-hare stories*, my little antennae go up in terms of wondering if DFOs are occurring.

Back to BCs

Back to the BCs phenomenon as a whole. Youth who fall into either of these two categories (BSC or BPC) do not look blatantly *crazy,* if you will. They do not have a florid thought disorder. They are not hallucinating. They are not delusional. But, their perceptual filters are caked over with gunk, in a sense. The perceptions of people and events around them are not the same as yours and mine. And again, BPCs' perceptual filters are *more seriously* gunked over than those of BSC.

> Youth who fall into either of these two categories (BSC or BPC) do not look blatantly *crazy, if you will...But, their perceptual filters are caked over with gunk...*

Another facet of a BC is that these youth do not even always outwardly **appear** odd or unusual. Yes, they almost exclusively are acting in hellion-like fashion – exhibiting tantrums and oppositionalism pell-mell. However, these youngsters frequently are not perceived as *strange*. The percentage who *do*, exclusively rest within the BPC camp. On the other hand, "Houston, we have a *problem...*"

As I say, some of the behaviors common to an underlying BC are: frequent ballistic episodes/tantrums *out-of-the-blue*, fierce oppositionalism, verbal as well as physical aggression, strange statements/questions, and *wild-hare* stories.

As indicated above, there are three BC *calling-cards*. The first is a *mild perceptual distortion*. The second is *a subtle thought disorder*. The third is *deviant fantasy operations* (or in *Plebian Latin* – a deviant fantasy life).

> Another facet of a BC is that these youth do not even always outwardly **appear** odd or unusual.

Now, if I am a child or teen within the throes of a BC, I might be exhibiting one, two, or *all three* of the above manifestations. It is not required that a youth display the entire threesome in order to be diagnosed with a BC. Obviously, however, a youngster **with** all three suffers a greater chance of being identified BPC, as opposed to the less severe BSC.

Summary

The Borderline Condition of Childhood (BC) manifests itself as: (1) a mild perceptual distortion; (2) a subtle thought disorder; and/or (3) deviant fantasy operations. In youth this syndrome is rarely blatant from an *overt* standpoint. Thus, it's not as if we see the *Loch Ness* poking his head up through the surface of the water. The intermittent nature of BC symptoms leaves parents, siblings, peers, and teachers never knowing when a behavioral explosion will come. And, they are highly frustrated and perplexed as to what is occurring with the child.

Chapter 10

"May Day! May Day!": Bipolar Variants

Perhaps no other mental condition of our day stirs up more controversy than Childhood Bipolar Disorder. Some have strongly questioned whether this syndrome even exists. In my view, however, this condition is clearly valid. I, on the other hand, believe that Childhood Bipolar Disorder is over-identified. Such has become the Designer Diagnosis of the 90s – and now on into the new millennium – much like ADHD in the 80s, wherein virtually every behavioral malady on the part of a youngster was ascribed *to* ADHD – at which point Ritalin became the nationwide panacea for emotionally disturbed youth.

Bipolar Types

There are 2 main types of *adult onset* Bipolar. The first is known as Bipolar I; such is a cycling between periods of mania followed by bouts of depression. During the manic stage, a person may present with pressured speech (words tumbling out on top of one another). There will often be a decreased need for sleep. The person is impulsive. There is grandiose thinking. On the other hand, the depressive

> [Childhood Bipolar Disorder] has become the Designer Diagnosis of the 90s – and now on into the new millennium – much like ADHD in the 80s...

stage entails frequent crying spells, a horribly depressed mood, and possibly suicidal thoughts.

In Bipolar II (for adults), an individual suffers mainly from depression, along with less frequent bouts of hypomania. Hypomania is an excited state accompanied by elevation of mood, distractibility, increased activity, and pressured speech. It is simply not as pronounced as a bona fide *mania*. These persons, while not experiencing the extreme highs and lows of Bipolar I, also tend to be irritable and agitated.

Cyclothymic Disorder is a much less malevolent *kissing-cousin* to Bipolar I and II. Here, an adult alternates between hypomania and depression; however, the highs and lows are not nearly as extreme. As we will see, however, Childhood Bipolar Disorder is a very different sea creature, from that of adult Bipolar.

Neuropsychologic Markers of Childhood Bipolar

I have thus far found seven markers of Childhood (or Adolescent) Bipolar by way of the neuropsychologic examination. They are: (1) Borderline Syndrome of Childhood; (2) Borderline Psychosis of Childhood; (3) neuropsychologic dysfunction; (4) emotionality via psychometric data; (5) rapid daily cycling/extreme moodiness; (6) chronic irritability; and (7) a parental history of Bipolar Disorder. Satisfying at least four of these criteria generally is consistent with a Childhood Bipolar variant of some sort. The seven markers are listed in the table below (Figure 10.1).

Markers of Childhood Bipolar Disorder

- Borderline Syndrome of Childhood
- Borderline Psychosis of Childhood
- Neuropsychologic Dysfunction
- Emotionality via Psychometric Data
- Rapid Daily Cycling/Extreme Moodiness
- Chronic Irritability
- Parental History of Bipolar Disorder

Figure 10.1 Markers for Childhood Bipolar Disorder

When Mark's work-up comes back with less than four of the seven signs of Bipolar, I am then generally dubious that this particular syndrome is lying on his ocean floor. An exception to that, however, is a three-item *combo plate* consisting of: (5) rapid daily cycling/extreme moodiness; (6) chronic irritability; and (7) a parental history of Bipolar. Whenever these three criteria are present – regardless of whether numbers one through four surface – I have learned over the years that a CBD is usually present.

Similar Disorders to Bipolar

Even so, a caveat must be mentioned, inasmuch as there **are** four other disorders that can produce a very similar neuropsychologic profile to that of Childhood Bipolar: (1) a Borderline Condition of Childhood in general; (2) Childhood Schizophrenia; (3) Major Depressive Disorder of Childhood with Psychotic or Borderline Psychotic Features; and (4) a budding Schizotypal Personality Disorder. Consequently, Bipolar conditions can be tricky to accurately diagnose in young persons.

The one saving grace though is that all but #1 (Borderline Conditions of Childhood) are rare to see in youngsters – even #3 (Major Depressive Disorder). Thus, if Heather satisfies **either set** of Childhood Bipolar criteria (the *Four of Seven Rule*, or the *Five, Six, and Seven Rule*), it is likely that this disorder is at least **one** below-the-water-line root cause producing her behavioral mayhem.

Four Syndromes with Similar Neuropsychologic Features

to Childhood Bipolar Disorder

(1) Borderline Condition of Childhood

(2) Childhood Schizophrenia

(3) Major Depressive Disorder of Childhood with

      Psychotic or Borderline Psychotic Features

(4) Budding Schizotypal Personality Disorder

Figure 10.2   Four Comparative Syndromes

What about these other four syndromes? Let's take a brief look at each.

(1) *Borderline Condition of Childhood*

If you will remember from Chapter 9, a Borderline Condition of Childhood (BC) is present when a youth satisfies any one of these three:

    ▷ a mild perceptual distortion;

    ▷ a subtle thought disorder; and/or

⊳ deviant fantasy operations.

Chapter 9 discusses BC in further detail.

(2) *Childhood Schizophrenia*

This serious genetically-induced mental disorder does not typically appear in most persons until their late teens/early 20s. But occasionally such can be seen among children and younger teens. Some of the signs of Schizophrenia are:

⊳ a florid thought disorder which may or may not include delusional beliefs

⊳ auditory (and/or more rarely) visual hallucinations

⊳ disorganized speech patterns (driven by a florid thought disorder)

⊳ extreme anxiety and fearfulness

⊳ impoverished interpersonal relationships – often replete with self-isolation

⊳ *bargain-basement* personal hygiene

⊳ chronic amotivation/lassitude/malaise.

(3) *Major Depressive Disorder of Childhood with Psychotic or Borderline Psychotic Features*

Youngsters who are struggling with MDD of Childhood display intense dysphoria (overt depression). Their behavior can be explosive and/or aggressive, self-destructive, unfocused and inattentive, and/or oppositional. Parents usually also see abrupt changes in appetite and sleep patterns. Moreover, these kiddoes may moreover present with confused thinking/mental processing.

(4) *Schizotypal Personality Disorder (incipient stages)*

This is in many aspects merely a much less malignant nephew to Schizophrenia. A *card-carrying* feature of this syndrome is a distinct personal *oddity*. That is, these youth impress others with a patent *strangeness* (e.g., mannerisms, dress, hygiene, topics of conversation, etc). Additional material regarding this disorder is contained in Chapter 12.

Description of Neuropsychologic Markers

As I mentioned before, there are seven markers which, in my experience, help diagnose Childhood Bipolar Disorder as gleaned from the neuropsychologic exam. To briefly re-state, they are:

(1) Borderline Syndrome of Childhood
(2) Borderline Psychosis of Childhood
(3) Neuropsychologic Dysfunction
(4) Emotionality via Psychometric Data
(5) Rapid Daily Cycling/Extreme Moodiness
(6) Chronic Irritability
(7) Parental History of Bipolar Disorder

The first two are: (1) Borderline Syndrome of Childhood; and (2) Borderline Psychosis of Childhood. As you will remember from the previous chapter, both have to do with: (1) a mild perceptual distortion; (2) a subtle thought disorder; and (3) deviant fantasy operations. The two conditions are similar, although they differ in *degree* – with BPC being of greater severity than BSC.

The third marker is neuropsychologic dysfunction. In everyday Portuguese, this refers to various and sundry markers of *potentially* aberrant brain function, gleaned from our battery of procedures – usually involving three or more abnormal neuropsychologic test results.

Next, emotionality via psychometric data is fourth. Emotionality (generally depression and/or anxiety) can be revealed on any of the various objective personality measures within the battery (generally the PIC, TAT-GA, and Rorschach).

In addition, rapid daily cycling/extreme moodiness is almost always a component of Childhood Bipolar. This refers to the highs (mania/hypomania) and lows (depression) through which the youth cycles back and forth, on a daily basis. The child or adolescent seems to surf a wave of elevated mood, then rapidly crashes into a sea of irritability or dysphoria. This rising and falling of mood/behavior is extremely taxing on parents, to say the least.

Chronic irritability is sixth. Here, the youth appears to be within the throes of almost constant irascibility, usually at least 70% of the child's waking life. Everything seems to grate on him. And, he is a *pill* to live with. Parents and siblings resonate with a sensation of having to *walk on egg-shells* around these kids.

Lastly, a positive family history of Bipolar Disorder is very significant, especially a *parental* history of such. Heredity is frequently a major player in its diagnosis. The probability of a child or grandchild being Bipolar after this disorder has occurred within the previous two generations is much greater than the general population – 15 to 30% more likely – as compared to only 4 to 6% *without* a family history of Bipolar (Child & Adolescent Bipolar Foundation, 2000).

> Chronic irritability... [manifests as] almost constant irascibility, usually at least 70% of the child's waking life.

Medications

Up until recently Lithium has been the gold standard for Bipolar treatment. But within recent years, anti-convulsants have **also** proven to be effective mood stabilizers. Parenthetically, my experience with one of the newer anti-convulsants, Lamictal, has been the **most** favorable. I see what appears to be a better addressment of any depressive aspects associated with Childhood/Adolescent Bipolar Disorder (CBD). Moreover, this agent – in short – appears to simply *work better* in terms of overall mood stabilization than the other anti-convulsants I have seen, when applied toward CBD.

Summary

Although Childhood Bipolar Disorder is not, in my opinion, nearly as prevalent as some in my field believe, such constitutes a very serious piece of refuse on the ocean floor, when present. Sort of like a 500-pound hammerhead shark. When it's there, it's **there**. And it has to be reckoned with. Moreover, failing to address this syndrome pharmacologically is much like swimming with a hammerhead.

Chapter 11

50 Fathoms Deep: Emotional Disturbance

Other common globs of toxic matter that can be dredged from the bottom of the bay for struggling youth are our old adversaries: depression and anxiety. These broad categories of emotionality, as will be described below, can be both vexing and covert for children and teens.

Depression

What is one thing we know about depression in youth? It is, more often than not, tricky to diagnose. Back in the early years of my career, working with adults, I had to be having a really, *really* bad day to miss depression in a grown-up. In fact, it would take me all of about 7 minutes, if that, once the individual sat down on the couch. The person *looked* sad. He wasn't eating. He wasn't sleeping. He had suicidal thoughts. I really had to be virtually brain-dead to miss a clinical depression in an adult.

> ...youth have their own unique displays of [depression].

Will a youth, such as Mark, display these same manifestations of depression as an adult (i.e., poor appetite, restlessness, sadness, insomnia, etc)? Well, sometimes he will. Unfortunately, in my experience, such is the minority of cases. Very often, youth have their own unique displays of this troubling emotion. So what does a depressed child or teen look like and do? He more typically shows this syndrome through crotchety behavior: oppositionalism, physical/verbal aggression, moodiness, chronic peer problems, and so forth (Gray, 1989).

Fortunately, markers of depression, as well as anxiety, in young persons can show up on a number of our tests: Trails A, WISC-III, Gordon, Littauer, PIC, TAT-GA, and Rorschach (see Chapter 21 for further discussion).

Another common factor is a family history of depression, and/or alcoholism. Frequently, a child will have strong cravings for junk-food/refined sugar, constituting an unwitting attempt to self-medicate the underlying depression. Alcohol and drug abuse are considered to be other means in which persons consciously or unconsciously attempt to self-medicate this biochemical disorder. Furthermore, among depressed teenage girls, sexual promiscuity is not uncommon. Any time I see this sort of overt behavior in an adolescent female, I suspect a possible covert depression.

> If we are able to identify a child with world-class oppositionalism – also suffering from depression, and we **neutralize** said depression – what then typically happens to at least a *portion* of the turmoil? Such should decrease, shouldn't it? It almost always **does**.

If we are able to identify a child with world-class oppositionalism – also suffering from depression, and we **neutralize** said depression –

93

what then typically happens to at least a *portion* of the turmoil? Such should decrease, shouldn't it? It almost always **does**. Thus, an additional factor to remember is that this syndrome can also make other disorders – such as ADHD or ODD – much worse than they *have* to be.

Types of Depression

In terms of the various sea-life depicting this condition, there are several: Anaclitic, Dysthymia, Masked, Major Depressive Disorder, etc).

Anaclitic Depression (AD) refers to a chronic condition seen within the infant/toddler population. These children are characterized by a listlessness, lassitude, or malaise – replete with blunted or flat affect (demeanor). Frequently AD is thought to be precipitated by neglect, abuse, and/or parental abandonment. Foreign or- phanages wherein less than ideal nurturance occurs, are filled with infants who appear to be anaclitically depressed.

> Dysthymia is simply the 25-cent term for *chronic depression.*

Dysthymia is simply the *25-cent* term for *chronic depression.* Chronic is defined as lasting 6 months or more. Here, many of the classic adult-like symptoms of this syndrome *are* seen in such kiddoes (overt sadness, crying, poor appetite, insom- nia, suicidal behavior, irritability, difficulty concentrating, etc). Thus, Dysthymic Disorder (DD) among youth is the *type* that most looks like typical **adult** depression. Frequently, this form occurs among youngsters with heavy genetic loadings of depression, or family histo- ries of alcohol/drug abuse.

Masked Depression is referred to as Atypical Depression, De- pressive Disorder NOS (Not Otherwise Specified), or *smiling depres- sion.* Much of the depression we see in youth constitutes the *masked* variety. Why? Because, as discussed above, more often than not, these youngsters display *their* depression in an atypical or masked way (oppositionalism, rebellion, boredom, poor school performance, etc).

Major Depressive Disorder (MDD) is considered to be the most severe form of the syndrome. Extreme helplessness, hopelessness, and profound sadness usually result in vegetative signs (sleep and appetite disturbance), suicidal fantasies/desires, lethargy, along with a horrid sense of gloom. Fortunately, MDD is the easiest form of depression to **treat**, oddly enough, for it generally responds very well to pharmacotherapy. And, it usually responds quickly – within 4 to 6 weeks. Moreover, such is true across the lifespan – from children to the elderly.

> Major Depressive Disorder is...the most severe form of depression... MDD is [however] the easiest form of depression to **treat**...

Anxiety

Just as there are different categories for depression, there are also aquatic permutations of anxiety: Generalized Anxiety Disorder, Phobic Disorder, Separation Anxiety, Post-traumatic Stress Disorder, etc.

Generalized Anxiety Disorder (GAD), a pervasive condition, is not always based on actual circumstances a person is facing. Sometimes GAD can be loosely characterized as *free-floating* anxiety. Common fears focus on upcoming events, and/or the thought of embarrassing oneself. Symptoms for children may include irritability, difficulties concentrating, low self-esteem, problems sleeping, and feeling overly tense.

Phobias can also plague youth. These are irrational fears related to an activity, place, or object which are excessive and/or unreasonable. Such may include the simple variety (dread of a specific object or situation – such as spiders, or the dark), agoraphobia (an aversion to being in public), and social phobias (fear of being humiliated or embarrassed in situations such as public speaking). School phobias are most common among youth, however.

On the other hand, among physically or sexually abused adolescents, a phobia may develop toward the gender of person who maltreated them. For example, a young girl who was violated by an adult male, or males, may avoid at all costs being alone with *anyone* of the masculine persuasion, no matter how safe she would otherwise be. Her anxiety sky-rockets when in the presence of males, due to the past abuse.

Separation Anxiety manifests when the child is temporarily removed from parent-figures, often resulting in panic or tantrums. Other signals that a kiddo is struggling with Separation Anxiety are frequent illnesses that require the youngster to remain with the care-giver (i.e., stomachaches, headaches, etc); does not attend sleep-overs or other age-appropriate activities due to fearfulness; wants to keep a parent in sight at all times; and literally clings to her mom or dad when feeling anxious (developing something of a *second-skin* phenomenon to the parent).

Panic Disorder is usually accompanied by distress attacks (increased heart rate/respiration, sweating, sudden/intense fear, etc). Often a child will scream, throw objects, and otherwise lose control of himself. The focus of said fear may not seem appropriate to an *adult*, but it is very real to the youngster. Panic Disorder is also thought to possess a heavy genetic component.

> Panic Disorder is... accompanied by... (increased heart rate/respiration, sweating, sudden/ intense fear...).

Post-traumatic Stress Disorder (PTSD) gained notoriety during and following the Viet Nam War. In World Wars I and II, symptoms of this condition were known as *Battle Fatigue, Combat Neurosis,* and

Shell-Shock. History buffs recall General George S. Patton, during the Second World War, publicly flagellating two separate G.I.s, ensconced within army field hospitals in Italy, suffering from what would later be monikered PTSD (during the Viet Nam era).

Among youth, PTSD frequently comes as fall-out to medical/emotional neglect, physical and/or sexual abuse (Gray, 1989). These kiddoes, as a result of such, can experience any or all of the following: night terrors, startle responses, insomnia, general nervousness, excessive (or deteriorated) appetite, food hoarding, bedwetting, fecal soiling, etc.

> [PTSD] kiddoes...can experience... night terrors, startle responses, insomnia, general nervousness, excessive (or deteriorated) appetite, food hoarding, bedwetting, fecal soiling, etc.

For children suffering from PTSD, it is extremely important that they perceive themselves to be in a safe environment. Additionally, directive play therapy can be helpful for such youth. And, various medications can also alleviate severe symptoms of anxiety.

Obsessive-Compulsive Disorder (OCD) is characterized by seemingly senseless/rigid behaviors which interfere with one's daily functioning. Think *Monk*, the "Defective Detective." For instance, a youth might wash her hands over and over, causing

> Obsessive-Compulsive Disorder is characterized by seemingly senseless/rigid behaviors...Think *Monk*, the "Defective Detective."

chronic skin irritation. Another young person might check and re-check the doors/windows, ensuring such are locked. OCD is another disorder believed to contain a heavy genetic predisposition. SSRIs are generally efficacious in treating this disorder. Cognitive/behavioral psychotherapy can also be helpful.

Oppositional Behaviors

Three other common disorders, frequently *linked* to emotionality, exist for children: Disruptive Behavior Disorder NOS (DBD), Oppositional Defiant Disorder (ODD), and Conduct Disorder (CD). DBD is the least severe of the three. A child with this syndrome often argues, loses his temper, annoys others, ignores rules/boundaries set up for him, and refuses to take responsibility for his own misdeeds.

> A child with this syndrome often argues, loses his temper, annoys others, ignore rules/boundaries...

Oppositional Defiant Disorder (ODD) is, in essence, merely a more severe/recalcitrant *mutant* of DBD.

I know. This description sounds like most *any* red-blooded *Amurican* adolescent, but behaviors associated with DBD or ODD must occur on a regular basis, create serious problems for the teen/family, *and* be present for 6 months or more in order to be diagnosable. Youth with a Choleric temperament (see Chapter 8) – paired with neglect, abuse or other

> Conduct Disorder... encompasses all the above, with additional dead-fish stench: property destruction, theft, aggression... along with *serious* legal violations.

mental health disorders – are at high risk for DBD or ODD, as are kiddoes with RAD (see Chapter 13).

Conduct Disorder (CD) encompasses all the above, with additional *dead-fish* stench: property destruction, theft, aggression toward people and/or animals, along with *serious* behavioral violations (shop-lifting, vandalism, etc) – often requiring legal/jurisprudence involvement. CD is likewise often accompanied by other mental health disorders (such as Major Depressive Disorder, Substance Abuse, Borderline Conditions of Childhood, etc).

Summary

Fortunately, most common emotionality disorders among youth are highly treatable – via behavioral interventions, pharmacotherapy, EEG Neurofeedback, and counseling. Chapters 14, 15, 16, and 19 discuss these options.

Chapter 12

Toxic Spills:
Character Pathology

In addition to temperaments, there is another ocean-born creature that drives behavior – character pathology – sometimes referred to as *characterologic features*, or *Personality Disorders*. As with psychologic make-up, such constitute long-lasting and enduring tendencies – resistant to change. It is important to note that a full-blown character pathology, or Personality Disorder, usually does not fully crystallize until the mid-teens.

Narcissism

From the neuropsychologic assessment, we can determine if there is a faint, or **strong**, aroma of Narcissism wafting through the sea mist. This syndrome is like unto the maelstrom at the bottom of the ocean that **may** be driving Mark's bossiness, defiance, failure to follow instructions, constant lying, etc.

A strong self-entitlement attitude is almost always lurking down in the abyss, as well. Here, Mark sees himself as *special* or *privileged*. Hence, the youngster will metaphorically mimic the lyrics of the late great crooner, Frank Sinatra, from the old hit, "I Did It **My** Way-ee."

Mark will often be greatly troubled as to how authority figures around him (parents, teachers, etc) could *possibly* expect that rules be followed, that homework/chores are done. What sort of unmitigated suffering are these adults seeking to inflict here anyway?

> A strong self-entitlement attitude is almost always lurking down in the abyss, as well...with Narcissism.

Sadly, the presence of Narcissism is not an earth-shattering revelation. It is particularly pervasive among the youth **I** see, given these youngsters' early years of narcissistic injuries (i.e., chaotic family of origin, neglect, abandonment, physical/sexual abuse, multiple placements, etc). In addition, a sequela for such a youth is that his *conscience* will usually appear lean – oftentimes for many years, unless he receives appropriate treatment.

Histrionic

This trait may also be found among youth. Typical sorts of Histrionic coral and fauna consist of psychologic immaturity, a demand for attention, and melodrama. Repeated suicidal gesturing is also common with these kiddoes. Histrionics furthermore correlates with interpersonal superficiality, as well as somatization tendencies (stress-related physical symptoms of one sort or another).

An over-utilization of the defense mechanisms of repression (the non-

> Typical sorts of Histrionic coral and fauna consist of psychologic immaturity, a demand for attention, and melodrama.

conscious *stuffing in* of uncomfortable/painful emotions/thoughts), is also common within the Histrionic matrix. Such is also true for suppression (the **conscious** *stuffing in* of same). As a result of suppression or repression, Heather may develop a pattern of ongoing/intermittent stomach pain. But frequent visits to the physician turn up nothing in terms of an underlying cause.

At any rate, Histrionic young persons may exhibit *some* or *all* of the above traits/symptoms.

Borderline

Borderline Personality Disorder (BPD) is best characterized as life *gone south* on an angry North Atlantic Sea. Recall the movie, *The Perfect Storm*? These Gloucester, Massachusetts men (George Clooney, et al) are – in a quest for a *Four-Star* fishing yield – wildly thrown about in their boat while braving an historically rip-roaring storm, maxing out the Richter Scale. Such is a great visual image of BPD. **(Recall that this syndrome is *not* synonymous with Borderline Conditions of Childhood/Adolescence; see Chapter 9.)**

The Perfect Storm... is a great visual image of BPD.

If Heather suffers with BPD, she will fluctuate from feeling that life is wonderful and full of excitement, to believing that all is lost due to someone's grievous slighting of her. This adolescent overreacts to very common situations in life (e.g., a friend who is late or needs to change plans). Obviously, it is immensely difficult for Heather to maintain friendships. She constantly struggles with notions of perceived rejection.

Borderline individuals usually portray a large chunk of Histrionics as part and parcel of their clinical presentations, as well. Common characteristics are chronic anger/hostility, disturbed interpersonal relationships, identity distortion, self-destructive behavior, and sexual acting out. The *fatal attraction* syndrome can also be part and parcel of Borderline character pathology.

Passive-Aggressive

The Passive-Aggressive trait typically rears its ugly head as an indirect, or *under-the-table*, means of discharging *anger*. Common examples of such among youth are: chronic lolly-gagging/procrastination (via homework, chores, etc); frequent tattling on peers/siblings; Academic Underachievement (in the face of capable intellect/skills); frequent lying/stealing; sabotage of family outings; *broken-record* sarcasm; ongoing *sneakiness*; etc.

> A Passive-Aggressive youngster often manifests a façade of apparent compliance, rather than an *overt* display of hostility.

A Passive-Aggressive youngster often manifests a façade of apparent compliance, rather than an *overt* display of hostility.

Dependent

The Dependent trait arises with a youth who excessively relies on other people to make decisions for him, requiring constant reassurance and approval from parent figures. Furthermore, because he lacks the self-esteem necessary to be assertive and decisive, conscious and/or non-conscious fears of being rejected are also present.

He typically shies away from new situations. This youth is a follower. Obviously then, there is much risk for trailing after *ne'er-do-well* peers into a perilous sunken ship – teetering on the edge of an underwater cliff (i.e., truancy, stealing, vandalism, *you-name-it*).

Schizotypal

Schizotypal individuals emit behavioral oddities. They also exhibit unusual perceptual experiences. In short, these youth impress as *strange*. Florid psychoses under stressful conditions can also develop. Many of her habits (poor hygiene, odd mannerisms, somewhat off-the-wall verbiage, etc) put others off – not exactly the way to win friends and influence people, at *any* age, much less during adolescence.

Compulsive

The Compulsive youth is obsessed with rule-keeping, details, and rigid structure. This young person often appears to be tightly *wound*. Frequently, she spends more time compiling itemized lists than actually accomplishing anything. Therefore, procrastination is as common as multi-colored scissor fish off the Káanapali shoreline of Maui. In addition, this kiddo tends to look at the world through a black and white lens. Shades of gray have no place in reality.

> Frequently, she spends more time compiling itemized lists than actually accomplishing anything.

Thus, personal rigidity is a common *calling-card*. Shifting gears, changing plans is extremely taxing for these youth.

Summary

Various character pathologies can be revealed via the neuropsychologic assessment. Specific tests in this regard are discussed in detail via Chapter 21. Although such personality disorders tend to be change-resistant among adults, with youth the prognosis is much better. Thus, there **are** ways to tame this breed of sea monster. Part III of the book gives solutions. So, *full steam ahead, Matey!*

Chapter 13

Shipwreck:
Reactive Attachment Disorder

Reactive Attachment Disorder (RAD) is another one of those diagnoses where there is much confusion over *"Who's* on first," *"What's* on second," and *"I Don't Know's* on third." In a nutshell, this disorder rears its ugly head when the bonding between a child and primary caretakers is flawed. Such is typically the result of neglect, abuse, or parental abandonment. Because scores of books already exist which discuss RAD in great detail, I will just be providing an overview here – mainly pertaining to the neuropsychologic exam.

> [RAD] is typically the result of neglect, abuse, or parental abandonment.

Origins of RAD

This condition often stems from the sudden departure of a primary caretaker (subsequent to death, hospitalization, divorce, etc); inconsistency of child-care (i.e., successive placements within foster homes, multiple daycare providers); postpartum depression or other chronic illness on the part of a caregiver; unremitting household chaos; prenatal drug/alcohol use, etc. While not every foster or adoptive kiddo suffers from attachment difficulties, the very fact Heather is not with her family of origin (FOO) indicates that the capacity for normal bonding, at some level, has probably been at least *threatened.*

If a young child is placed into a loving home before the age of 6 months, the probability of finding RAD as part of the refuse on the ocean floor is greatly reduced. However, in the event a youngster is 6 months or older when removed from her family of origin, then attachment difficulties are at greater risk.

RAD kiddoes often develop a *faux* bonding. It is totally superficial, and oft-times related to the *Honeymoon Phase* of a newly placed maltreated youngster in adoption or foster care. Hence, the child appears to quickly bond with his new parents; but in reality, there is no *genuine* attachment. It is **all** superficial.

In an abusive family situation, Mark is often dependent – for his basic life needs – on the very adult who maltreats him. So while it makes no apparent sense for the kiddo to bond to the abusing grown-up, a dependence/bonding takes place nonetheless – a hostile-dependent relationship, or perhaps an *identification with the aggressor syndrome.*

But, this is only a survival technique (sometimes referred to as traumatic bonding) – not at all genuine or healthy. Such is evidenced when a child begs not to be taken from his family of origin, despite ongoing horrendous abuse and neglect.

The field of behavioral science has been aware of RAD long enough now that many time-tested variants of **respectful/gentle** Bonding/Attachment Therapy have been developed to help these youth. Plus, after 20 years of following these kids, I have had the opportunity to observe what works and what does not.

In addition to appropriate therapy, young persons with RAD must be in a safe, supportive, and loving environment – often for years – before the effects of the early trauma can be healed.

Remember, the youngster has been conditioned that adults cannot be trusted. This notion takes time to demolish. It is only through the consistent love, faithfulness, and trustworthiness of the foster/adoptive parents, along with appropriate Bonding/Attachment Therapy – as well as other cutting-edge treatments – that the child can risk opening up his heart again to others.

> ...children with RAD must be in a safe, supportive, and loving environment – often for years – before the effects of the early trauma can be healed.

Symptoms of RAD

Typical symptoms include: tenuous bonding with foster/adoptive parents, poor boundaries with strangers, superficiality *to the hilt*, frequent nocturnal wandering, food hoarding, animal cruelty, and wholesale manipulation of those who care about the child's well-being. Oppositionalism is world-class. Even the *French* judge agrees. Verbal/physical aggression, stealing, and *crazy lying* (falsehoods even in the face of observable evidence – Federici, 1998) are also common.

Additionally, RAD young persons possess a tremendous propensity for sabotaging their own progress in life. Moreover, they may engage in dangerous/risky conduct, seemingly without regard to potential consequences. Hence, safety issues are a prime concern with many such youth. These youngsters' conscience seems to get tangled up among seaweed and other underwater plant-life. Furthermore, such kiddoes almost invariably are academic underachievers.

RAD kiddoes often display a superficially charming demeanor, but only as a means of perfecting their skills firmly ensconced within the *M-word* (manipulation). I recall a recent publicized account of a youngster who charmed his way down the East Coast, informing car-

107

> RAD youth often display a superficially charming demeanor, but only as a means of perfecting their skills firmly ensconced within the *M-word* (manipulation).

ing adult strangers along the way that he had been tossed out by his parents, etc, etc. Come to find out, this was a boy with RAD who had gone AWOL from a loving family.

RAD young persons use skillful *maneuvering* in order to maintain as much governance over their world as possible. Control is the best insurance policy they have. Such insulates them from being hurt once again by adults. Therefore, these youth strive to keep all relationships on *their* terms.

Hence, it goes without saying that a RAD child's relationships with others are notoriously shallow. As I say, many of them can charm the skin off a Brazos River Water Moccasin. Young persons with RAD *distance* themselves from people in order to avoid the same kind of rejection they have suffered, earlier in life. More importantly, such young persons are almost invariably *All-Pro* Narcissists – lacking empathy for the needs of most other warm-blooded seafaring creatures.

> RAD youth *distance* themselves from people in order to avoid the same kind of rejection they have suffered, earlier in life.

It is very common to find RAD youth also suffering from other co-existing diagnoses. Common sailing partners are: Conduct Disorder, Oppositional Defiant Disorder, ADHD, and Borderline Conditions.

Psychotherapy with RAD Youth

For counseling to adequately address bonding issues, such must not exist in a vacuum. That is to say we must exorcise all the other swarming piranhas out of the Amazon, in order to best facilitate Bonding/Attachment Therapy.

But having *said* that, there is no *quick **cure*** for RAD. Trust must be rebuilt slowly over time. Duh. But, it is amazing how much progress *can* be made as we work with the whole child via a coordinated treatment plan. Such is, you might say, precisely why I *wrote* this book: unless a thorough neuropsychologic exam is conducted, the co-existing *crappola* of this youth's ocean floor is often missed.

For instance, if Heather suffers from a Borderline Psychosis of Childhood (BPC) – along *with* RAD – how will the two syndromes interact?

Glad you asked.

The BPC will make the RAD infinitely more recalcitrant. Said another way, if we can clean out the BPC muck from the bottom of the

> ...if we can clean out the BPC muck from the bottom of the sea...RAD becomes infinitely more *treatable*...

sea, then we have done Heather *and* her family a great service. Because now, the RAD becomes infinitely more *treatable* – praise God! The nice thing about a BPC, bizarre as this sounds, is that there are medications that can quickly drive it into remission. Now, **psychotherapy** progress with *RAD* can start to ***take off***.

Obviously, to best assist RAD youth, there needs to be trained folk in her life who can conduct the much needed attachment/bonding work. Persons in the field, to name only a **few**, who perform this type of highly specialized world-class therapy with RAD youth are: Greg Keck, Dan Hughes, Barbara Rila, Michael Pines, Beth Powell, Kathy Baczynski, Roxanne Whitford Shoulders, Connie Hornyak, and others.

I rely upon impeccably trained persons such as these, to offer up the psychotherapy piece of the puzzle needed in the treatment of RAD. Other excellent Bonding/Attachment therapeutic resources can be found via the ATTACh organization (Association for Treatment and Training in the Attachment of Children) – **www.attach.org**.

Parents of children with RAD often suffer *greatly* under the demanding load they bear. Frequently, hope is lost – dealing daily with the unscrupulous behaviors of their youngster. Unknowing Land Lubbers often wrongly judge the family dynamic and diagnose the cause of the problem as resting with the foster/adoptive parents. Unattached children are very helpful in encouraging this misconception via their aforementioned charming and engaging behavior when in the presence of others. Society's false blame toward loving parent figures only makes the situation that much more maddening. However, such is pure, unmitigated ignorance.

> A further mistake is a belief in the premise that unconditional love will cure *all*. "If I just love this child enough, he will come around." Were it that simple.

A further mistake is a belief in the premise that unconditional love will cure *all*. "If I just love this child enough, he will come around." Were it that simple.

Brain Pathways

Severe attachment disorders *do* have neurologic gurglings. The more a brain region is used, the deeper the routes for that function become. Unfortunately what happens with attachment disorders is that neuronal pathways for stress, survival, and fear become ingrained, usually buried within the brain – involving the amygdala (memory), limbic system (emotions), etc.

Thus, neurologic consequences are often apathy, anger, an underdeveloped conscience, impulsivity, aggression, and depression, *ad infinitum, ad nauseam*. Given that the body/brain is in a constant heightened alert mode during chronic psychologic trauma, neurobiology changes. And not for the better.

Summary

RAD requires much patience to overcome the horrific attachment difficulties that arise from early childhood neglect/abuse. On an encouraging note, the brain *is* capable of re-establishing pathways. Good, consistent, nurturing relationships – as well as direct brain intervention (see EEG Neurofeedback, Chapter 15) along with other state-of-the-art treatments – can resurrect the shipwreck that is RAD.

The Maltreated Child

Part III

Cleaning Out the Canal

Chapter 14

Call in the Coast Guard: Medication Options

Do you remember the 1980s? I do. A few years back, I not so affectionately dubbed the 80s *The Decade of ADHD*.

Why?

Well, because many mental health professionals in the U. S. of A. were finding ADHD in every pond, stock tank, and channel. I recall in the large metropolitan area where I lived and practiced at the time, there was a pediatric mental health clinic notorious for diagnosing every child who entered there as ADHD – shortly after coming through the front entrance. Then the youth invariably (or so it seemed) emerged out the back door clutching a script for Ritalin.

Anyway, I spent a goodly portion of the 80s performing thorough work-ups on many of these same children, only to discover that ADHD either was not a player, or was at best a cameo performer. (This was after boatloads of parents had brought in scores of youngsters to our clinic, for purposes of figuring out what the underlying root causes were for all their continued behavioral mayhem – subsequent to the psychostimulant not working.)

Do I believe ADHD is a viable clinical syndrome? Absolutamatory. I simply found that it *didn't* lurk under every rock, like unto a McCarthy Era communist.

The Golden Age of Bipolar

Then came the 1990s. I regard the 90s (and continuing into the new millennium) as *The Golden Age of Bipolar*. Now, we are finding *Bipolar* under every rock. And with that, come a slew of mood/impulse stabilizers, usually in the form of anti-convulsant meds.

Having *said* that, I do believe in the validity of Childhood Bipolar Disorder – just not with every incoming tide.

All the Way to the *TOP*

Most of us as parents and professionals have seen an all-too-common occurrence associated with medications and multiple diagnoses in maltreated kiddoes. I call it the TOP (*Tack-On Phenomenon*).

TOP happens when, after each RTC admission, the child in question has another, and then yet another psychotropic *tacked on*. After five or six different psychiatrists, the youngster has accrued five or six medications. Why aren't some of these meds taken away? Obviously the youth is receiving little benefit from them – or else he wouldn't continue to so massively *struggle* in life.

I don't want to give the wrong impression, however. There *are* children besieged with RAD along with other serious psychopathology who simply cannot live without appropriate and reasonable medication therapy as part of their treatment plans.

The emphasis here however

> My job as a pediatric neuropsychologist is to: (1) hear where the parents *are*; and then (2) lay out the smorgasbord of psychotropic options…

should be on *appropriate and reasonable.*

Using Medications

My approach with parents? I see my duty as laying out the options – in terms of possible medications for their kiddoes (along with behavioral and academic strategies). Parents generally rest within one of three groupings: (1) those who are anti-meds; (2) those who are pro-meds; and (3) those who are ambivalent.

My job as a pediatric neuropsychologist is to: (1) hear where the parents *are*; and then (2) lay out the smorgasbord of psychotropic options, based upon the neuropsychologic blue-print of their particular child or teen. We then thoroughly examine the pros and cons of each.

Thus, the use of medication is not my call. Nor is it *my* right to make this call. It is the *parents'* right, in cooperative synchrony with their physician. If I can emotionally support the parents, perform a comprehensive exam of their son or daughter, and then articulate to them what the options are – along with the associated pros and cons – then I have done my job.

Yes, I *do* cringe when a youth comes into me bathed in obvious polypharmacy. And yes, I *am* disgusted when medications are abused. But, anything can be abused: religion, physical exercise, nutrition, and – pharmacology. Let's not throw the baby out with the seawater.

How many times have I seen a child struggling with a nasty case of RAD, flower-up and improve, by virtue of an effective treatment plan which included the judicious use of medications? (Answer: a *bunch*.) The end result was that the youngster's little neurochemical aquarium was hosed out and cleansed. Then, attachment therapists and other members of the treatment team could do *their* jobs.

The moral of this story: There *is* hope – even for the most difficult youth. Let's use everything here on earth God has given us to help these troubled children – including medications.

But let's use them well.

Your Personal Consultant

I see my job as a *consultant*. Just as a dietitian looks at the nutritional value of a client's food intake, I, too, examine the various factors influencing the child. The kiddo's diagnosis, background situation, and general health issues all influence his behavior. Just as in the supermarket abide many different types of vegetables – each with its own vitamin and mineral combination – there are various treatment options for youth – each with its own benefits. Based on the NP data, I then provide the parents the necessary *nutritional information* they need in deciding which *vegetables* to serve their child.

> ...I then provide the parents the necessary *nutritional information* they need in deciding which *vegetables* to serve their child.

When a youngster comes into my clinic, one of the crucial bits of information I need is the most complete psychotropic history the parents can give. I ask which medications the young person has been on **previously**, how she fared on them, what the dosage levels were, how long she was **on** each, etc.

> Thus, knowing which Rxs have *not* worked narrows the field of efficacious medications – saving time, money, and migraines.

Thus, knowing which Rxs have *not* worked narrows the field of efficacious medications – saving time, money, and migraines. It is rare that we don't find *some* agent that is effective and makes life much more bearable for everyone concerned – the child, siblings, parents, peers, teachers.

Often, in the case of foster/adoptive kiddoes there is no possibility of finding out the who/what/when/where/why of past medications, duration/efficacy, etc. We just have to work with the information that is available. And that can be *done*. But each piece of the puzzle we *can* find, makes the picture a little clearer. So we gather up as much as possible. At times, this data is attainable from caseworker files.

Now, let's look at the most common agents used on behalf of maltreated youth.

ADHD Medications

There are three different types of medicines used to treat ADHD: psychostimulants, Beta-blockers, and anti-depressants. The one most commonly prescribed – that most people are familiar with, is psychostimulants.

Psychostimulants

Let us think about a stimulant here for a moment. What does this agent do to the central nervous system? It speeds it up – increases heart rate, blood pressure, etc. Recall from our discussion on ADHD (see Chapter 7) that overactive behavior from these children is often thought to be a result of their own attempts to self-stimulate sleepy pre-frontal lobes of their brains. At least, that is the most cogent current theory. We find that when this region of the cerebral cortex is neurochemically stabilized, the youngster often ceases the *self-stim* behaviors – and consequently calms down!

> We find that when this region of the cerebral cortex is neurochemically stabilized, the youngster often ceases the *self-stim* behaviors – and consequently calms down!

Ritalin, Dexedrine, Dextrostat, Adderall, Concerta, Metadate, and Cylert are all psychostimulants. When a child begins on one of these meds, we always start with a low-dose. Such can gradually be increased, until the appropriate level is reached.

Regarding side-effects of these medications, the primary *Nautical Hit Parade* is: (1) appetite suppression; (2) insomnia; (3) headaches; and (4) irritability. Now, many of the children brought in to me are *already* irritable; they don't need any *more* irritability! Side-effects may be short lived, lasting only the first couple of days as the child's body becomes accustomed to the medication. Or, such can be persistent, in which case we then need to shift gears and try another stimulant option.

As you are probably aware, one kiddo with ADHD will do marvelously on Ritalin, yet poorly on Adderall, or vice-versa. Often in the workshops I do, a mom sitting on the right side of the audience will say, "My son is doing *great* on Ritalin. It was as if someone flipped on a light switch for him – a complete and total change for the better!"

> ...odds are that if your kiddo *truly has* ADHD, and in the past was put on a Rx that did not work, there is one that *will*.

Inevitably however, a mother from the left side of the room will respond, "Well, Ritalin was a total bust for my Billy – no change at all! *Adderall* is what worked for us!" Hence, each youngster responds differently to medications – so it's a matter of finding out what works best for *your* son or daughter.

The good news though is that we have a wide selection of choices for this disorder. So, the odds are that if your kiddo *truly has* ADHD, and in the past was put on a Rx that did not work, there is one that *will*.

Beta-blockers

A second class of agents used to treat ADHD is low-dose Beta-blockers. Researchers and clinicians stumbled upon the fact that tiny doses of this agent are very effective with a subset of ADHD children. Beta-blockers' claims to fame are on two fronts: impulsivity and aggression. Therefore, if your ADHD youngster has either of these symptoms, there is a good chance that a Beta-blocker may be the best medication for **him** – frequently in combination with a low-dose psychostimulant. Clonidine and Tenex are the two brand-name Beta-blockers most commonly seen.

Anti-depressants (usage with ADHD)

The old tricyclic anti-depressants (especially Tofranil) have a long history of usage in the neutralization of ADHD symptoms. Within the last 15 years or so, newer vintage mood elevators however have almost exclusively taken the place of low-dose tricyclics by way of treating ADHD-related symptomatology (when psychostimulants and/or Beta-blockers are deemed undesirable).

The most **recent** development along the lines of anti-depressant as ADHD agent is seen with Strattera. Strattera is actually a Selective Norepinephrine Reuptake Inhibitor (SNRI). Thus far, it has been marketed as another **non-psychostimulant** ADHD treatment option for parents or physicians who are desirous of such. For a more detailed treatise of anti-depressant agents in general, see below.

Anti-depressants (as Mood Elevators)

The third group of medications used to treat ADHD is mood elevators. In fact, tricyclics have a fairly long history of serving in this manner. This old breed of anti-depressant was actually brought to the New World in 1843 by Moses on the Ark. (My knowledge of theological history is a little suspect; just bear *with* me here.) Some of the familiar drugs in this class are: Elavil, Tofranil, Pamelor, and Sinequan. As I say, these particular agents have been with us seemingly forever. Doctors would swear by them, because for adults they *worked*, and worked very well – for depression.

The problem with these older anti-depressants is that there are many side-effects – primarily sleepiness. So getting up in the morning can be a chore. Other unwanted spin-offs are cotton-mouth, nausea, dizziness, and headaches.

The next category of meds used to fight depression is the SSRIs (Selective Serotonin Reuptake Inhibitors): Prozac, Zoloft, Paxil, Luvox, and Celexa. The first, Prozac, came out in 1988. Many swear *by* it. Some swear *at* it.

Effexor is an agent that inhibits the reuptake of both Serotonin **and** Norepinephrine. Serzone (a Serotonin Antagonist and Reuptake Inhibitor – SARI) does the same, although its chemical structure is different from all other anti-depressants. Another agent is Wellbutrin (dubbed a Norepinephrine-Dopamine Reuptake Inhibitor – NDRI) whose claim to fame, in addition to being a mood elevator, is helping people lose weight and stop smoking. Moreover, among youth, Wellbutrin is considered by many to be the best anti-depressant by way of helping neutralize ADHD symptoms. At any rate, the non-tricyclic anti-depressants work better than tricyclics, and with fewer side-effects. So now, the non-tricyclic anti-depressants are the preferred first line of defense against depression.

> In the depressed person, as brain cells secrete neurotransmitters, these same tiny structures *take back* the neurotransmitters they have just released, thereby creating a *deserty* synapse.

How exactly do anti-depressants work in the brain? Basically, with psychotropic medications, all we have are theories, since we cannot actually dissect a working brain. The space between individual brain cells (see Figure 14.1) is called the synapse. And in these tiny gaps are substances, neurotransmitters, that allow cells to *talk to* one another, sending impulses from one to the next. You can think of neurotransmitters as the *juice* that *allows* cells to communicate. When someone is depressed, or anxious, the spaces between the various neurons become dry: sort of like a micro-slice of the Sahara Desert.

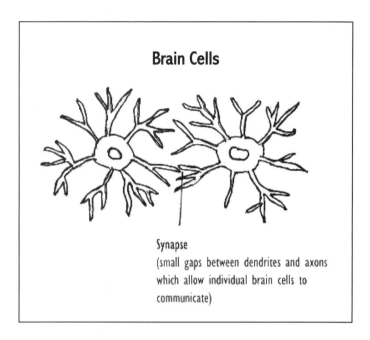

Brain Cells

Synapse
(small gaps between dendrites and axons
which allow individual brain cells to
communicate)

Figure 14.1 Synapse

In the depressed person, as brain cells secrete neurotransmitters, these same tiny structures *take back* the neurotransmitters they have just released, thereby creating a *deserty* synapse. One of these juices that is often taken back *in* by the releasing cells is Serotonin. Selective Serotonin Reuptake Inhibitors, then, arrest the reuptake – the process by which the neurons *take back* the chemical (neurotransmitters) they have just released. In this case, the particular *juice* is the Serotonin.

Some of the other juices which enable cells to communicate within our brain are Norepinephrine and Dopamine.

For many years, children who were displaying signs of depression or anxiety were given low-dose Tofranil. It was just about the only game in town for youth with a mood disorder. But now, with the advent of the SSRI agents, I find Paxil and Zoloft give us the best bang for our buck. At least, that is *my* opinion. The old Tofranil (sometimes referred to in its generic form – Imipramine) finishes in last place to the low-dose SSRIs in all ages, especially among children and teens. Again, my opinion.

Another footnote on Tofranil: some of you know this agent formerly was considered the medication of choice among a certain subset of ADHD youth. Frequently, Tofranil would be combined with a psychostimulant to best help a child. The anti-depressant is beneficial by stabilizing the *mood* among kiddoes who had both depression (and/or anxiety) on their plates – *as well as* ADHD.

> One of the beauties of SSRIs, when given in the low dosages needed for youngsters, is that side-effects are rare.

One of the beauties of SSRIs, when given in the low dosages needed for youngsters, is that side-effects are rare. In the unusual case wherein I *do* see a side-effect, what do you think it is? Sleepiness? Weight gain? Weight loss? Stomach problems?

No, the more typical outcome I see is a little bit of cotton-mouth. It *is* possible for these medications to dry the mucous membranes, ever so slightly, in the upper respiratory tract. But usually this only occurs the first 2 or 3 days the child is on it; then the dryness usually goes away, gets better, or is no longer bothersome.

Among practically all anti-depressants, *with 6 you get egg roll*. What I mean is that this type of agent is by definition a *mood elevator*.

But the bonus we get via the anti-depressant is its anxiolytic or, in *Poor Man's Greek, anti-anxiety* properties.

So, if I have a kiddo who is suffering from both a depression **and** an anxiety component – which is quite common, by the way, among the population of youngsters who have been maltreated – the anti-depressant will frequently help with *both*.

Another use of SSRI medications is for Borderline Conditions of Childhood (see Chapter 9). I have found that in about 50% of young persons 10 and below who have been diagnosed *with* a Borderline Condition of Childhood, a low-dose SSRI will send such into remission. (More discussion on this later in the chapter.)

> Another use of SSRI medications is for Borderline Conditions of Childhood.

Anxiolytics (Anti-anxiety Agents)

As stated above, the 25-cent name for anti-anxiety medications is *anxiolytic* agents. Feel free to drop this moniker at the next boring mixer you attend (especially if you are hopeful of being asked to leave early). Here again, we have older and newer types of anti-anxiety drugs.

The old favorites – also brought over by Moses on the Ark – are Valium (Vitamin V, as we call it) along with Librium. Serax is another. Ativan yet another. These medications are all very effective in reducing anxiety; the down-side is their addictive nature. Hence, they can only be used short-term. Furthermore, you will never (or very **rarely**) see them given to *children* who are suffering from anxiety.

Xanax is another anxiolytic medication. It came out around 1982. Touted as the first anti-anxiety med that was non-addictive, this assertion was patently false. It *is* addictive! In fact, back when I was working with adults – during my Dr. Bob Hartley-wannabe days – I would treat men who had been on Xanax for, say, a year – prescribed for General Anxiety Disorder (GAD). When it was apparent they were developing an addiction, we would begin to wean them *off* Xanax. They had the same clinical presentation as someone who had been abusing *alcohol* for a year – a seemingly very similar biochemical addiction.

BuSpar, on the other hand, is one of the newer anti-anxiety medicines on the market. Although technically an anti-depressant, this agent is almost universally thought of exclusively as an anxiolytic. BuSpar really *is* nonaddictive. It has been out long enough for us to know that one cannot get addicted to BuSpar even if you *work* at it. It is very benign.

Furthermore, if you need a life, and wish to stage a contest for the psychotropic with the lowest side-effect profile, BuSpar wins hands down. In fact, with adults, this agent has earned the reputation among psychiatrists, as "the medication in search of an indication." In other words, it is that *gentle*. Therefore, for a kiddo who is struggling with acute, or even a chronic/free-floating anxiety, BuSpar can be very effective, in my experience. Remember: (1) it is very mild; and (2) there are virtually no side-effects! What could be better for a **child**?!

Neuroleptics/Anti-psychotics

Neuroleptics and anti-psychotics are synonymous. But anti-psychotic has such an emotional charge to it that I rarely refer to these agents in this manner, at least while in the presence of parents. I prefer the term *neuroleptic*, because it does not carry the same malevolent connotation.

The first neuroleptic, Thorazine, takes us back once again to the time of Moses' arrival at Plymouth Rock. I am finding he brought quite the pharmacopoeia with him. At any rate, Thorazine was introduced in the year of my birth – 1953, revolutionizing the field of mental health overnight. Psychiatric hospitals all over the world could then stop using aversive physical restraints (the old *straight-jacket, e.g.*). This was the first neuroleptic to be manufactured. Other such agents which have been around almost as long are: Mellaril, Navane, Haldol, Prolixin, Moban, etc.

However, I have not personally seen a young person who has been on Thorazine, even at a low-dose, for a good 10 to 12 years now. About 2 years ago I was at a conference, and a mental health technician from Kentucky said, "We have a child in our RTC who is on Thorazine." This took me aback. Why? Because Thorazine is extremely cardiotoxic – even for adults. Furthermore, it can be very, very soporific – as well as cognitively *dulling*. Moreover, we now have infinitely better neuroleptics which are much safer.

> ...Thorazine was introduced in the year of my birth – 1953, revolutionizing the field of mental health overnight.

Think back to the movie, *One Flew Over The Cuckoos' Nest*, with Jack Nicholson, playing the inimitable scalawag, Randle McMurphy. McMurphy commits himself to the hospital to avoid working on a prison farm. He constantly locks horns with the charge-nurse – the sadistic Nurse Ratched, played by Louise Fletcher. Her goal is absolute control over the patients. McMurphy, on the other hand, is into doing his own thing, a veritable Narcissist on parade.

Unlike the rest of the men on the ward, McMurphy still laughs and smiles. At one point he tries to pull a fast one on his buddies; he acts as if he has had a pre-frontal lobotomy – replete with a scene in which he aptly displays the patented *Thorazine Shuffle*: a slumped posture as he slowly and methodically glides his feet down the hallway. The moral: Thorazine is rarely a good choice for kids.

Atypical Anti-psychotics/Neuroleptics

Fortunately, there is a new breed of neuroleptics which have proven a God-send for maltreated youth. Actually, the more precise term for these is *Atypical Anti-psychotics* – consisting of Risperdal, Zyprexa, Seroquel, Clozaril, Geodon, etc. Risperdal came out in the early 1990s. It is the one with which I have had the most success, partly due to its having been on the market longer than the others, perhaps.

Remember the old 1960s *Brille Cream* commercials: "A little dab'll *do* you"? Same is true with Risperdal. It generally only takes .5 to 1 mg of Risperdal a day to *drain the canal*, so to speak, for many kiddoes with a Borderline Condition. An older youngster might require up to 2 or 3 mg per day, depending upon the severity of the BC, etc.

If you remember, from earlier in this chapter, one of the uses I mentioned for the new SSRI anti-depressants is for youth with Borderline Conditions. But I have found that as a child gets older, the efficacy of a low-dose SSRI only works in about 25 to 50% of the youngsters with this condition. However, knowing a kiddo *has* a BC lurking on the ocean floor, we will start with a low-dose SSRI and play our odds, hoping for the best. If it works, the 200 lb. Marlin has been *caught*! If it *doesn't* work, then we go to plan B: a low-dose *atypical neuroleptic.*

Now, why try a low-dose SSRI (or similar new-breed anti-depressant) in lieu of just cutting to the chase with a low-dose neuroleptic? Because the side-effect profile of an SSRI, as well as other anti-depressants, is generally more benign than that of an atypical neuroleptic.

With the use of an atypical neuroleptic, I find in treating a Borderline Condition, that, in some cases, only 90 to 120 days are needed on this medication to get the child back on track. Other youth, with considerably *more* muck at the bottom of the lagoon need a longer regimen on it. The atypical neuroleptic helps restore normal brain chemistry. Such *cleans up the toxic underwater waste.*

These medications *can* require only a short-term regimen for a Borderline Condition to be driven out of Lake Erie. Other young persons may require a low-dose atypical neuroleptic for several years. It all depends on what is found via the neuropsychologic exam.

Moreover, I have found through the years that we can provide a great many things in *perfect* fashion for a young person: (1) Fred Rogers/Kelly Frey as tag-team psychotherapists;

> Moreover, I have found...that we can provide a great many things in *perfect* fashion for a young person: (1) Fred Rogers/Kelly Frey as tag-team psychotherapists; (2) Ivy League-quality academic instruction; (3) Bill Crosby as 24/7 phone-in parental consultant; and (4) June Cleaver as chief domestic engineer. However, all will be to little or no avail, unless we dredge a BC from the bottom of the reservoir.

(2) Ivy-League quality academic instruction; (3) Bill Cosby as 24/7 phone-in parental consultant; and (4) June Cleaver as chief domestic engineer. However, all will be to little or no avail, unless we dredge a BC from the bottom of the reservoir.

If I've learned anything at all over my 22 years in the mental health field, it's that treating a BC is **primary** to restoring a kiddo's *life*.

One reason why the newer atypical anti-psychotics are heralded by the medical community is their vastly reduced side-effect profile. Such is much lower than the older Thorazines, Mellarils, and Prolixins. With an atypical anti-psychotic for example, the risk for Tardive Dyskinesia, a chronic motor tic disorder, is greatly less. No question though that the most vexing spin-off of some of the atypical anti-psychotics is weight gain. But, the side-effect profile for these agents is *nothing*, compared to the old-guard/ *Moses-class* anti-psychotic agents.

Hypnotics (Soporifics)

The next category is hypnotics (soporific agents) – just a fancy term for medicines that induce sleep, or help treat insomnia. I hardly ever see a child on a free-standing hypnotic agent. I do, however, *frequently* get a youth on De-syrel (generic: Trazodone) for insomnia. This is yet another *New Breed* anti-depressant (*not* brought over by Moses to the New World in the mid 1800s). The most common side- effect of Desyrel is drowsiness (hence the rationale for its utility in inducing sleep). Therefore, it is given at h.s. (bedtime).

> If I've learned anything at all over my 22 years in the mental health field, it's that treating a BC is **primary** to restoring a kiddo's *life*.

Insomnia is almost always going to be a symptom of that highly astute and pedantic clinical entity I have identified as *something else.* So if a child *does* have trouble sleeping, I personally prefer to treat the underlying root cause of it. Common sources are: masked depression, PTSD, high doses of psychostimulants used to treat ADHD, etc.

> Insomnia is almost always going to be a symptom of... *something **else***.

Medicines used *solely* to induce sleep are Restoril (having just *missed* passage on the Ark with Moses), and Ambien. Halcion was also used back in the 1980s, but was pretty much forced to go the way of the White Buffalo, mainly due to fears of side-effects, some real – some perceived.

Another common medication

providing a soporific punch is the old-guard tricyclic anti-depressant, Elavil. But, similar to Restoril, Ambien, and Halcion – Elavil is typically used with adults. As Baby Boomers age, we notice a goodly proportion of our elderly parents being placed on low-dose Elavil (a Moses-class nuclear sub), frequently used as a soporific, to help them sleep better at night. If you ask your elderly parent what *kind* of med their Elavil is, they almost invariably have no idea it's an anti-depressant – "It just helps me *sleep*."

Anti-enuretic Agents

Given that enuresis is a problem most children outgrow, physicians generally prescribe medications for it only if the problem is chronic, and/or causing stress for the child and family. When needed, the most commonly used agent for enuresis is DDAVP (Desmopressin). This is an anti-diuretic compound in the form of a nasal spray or tablet which, in essence, inhibits the body's production of fluid during the night. The other, *older* alternative is Imipramine (trade name – Tofranil). Such in essence blocks the bladder from emptying during the night, due to its anti-cholinergic side-effects.

Anti-convulsants (Mood/Impulse Stabilizers)

The last category of psychotropics for us to consider is mood/impulse stabilizers. Here, the slate of options consist of: Tegretol, Neurontin, Depakote, Topamax, Lamictal, etc. Actually all of these are *anti-convulsant* medications – originally designed for folks who have epilepsy/seizure disorders. However, mood/impulse stabilizing properties *also* exist for anti-convulsants. Lithium is not a true anti-convulsant, but *is* used for the same purpose as Tegretol, et al – as a mood stabilizer.

Lithium Carbonate (LiCo) is actually a salt found in the earth. Serendipity (translated: *dumb luck*) led to the discovery that many persons who suffer from biochemically-driven undulations of mood – or poor impulse control – stabilize with the use of Lithium.

Formerly, Lithium was the sole treatment of choice for what we used to call *Manic-Depressive Illness* – now termed Bipolar Disorder. Bipolar is the cycling of moods wherein a person can go from the heights of grandeur and ecstasy to the depths of Hell and depression, back up again, then down, and so forth. Lithium has proven effective with a subset of youngsters who possess these radical mood swings, along with Depakote, Tegretol, Lamictal, Neurontin, etc.

> Formerly, Lithium was the sole treatment of choice for what we used to call *Manic-Depressive Illness* – now termed Bipolar Disorder.

An adolescent may be experiencing side-effects when taking Lithium if there are notable drowsiness, weakness, nausea, vomiting, fatigue or increased thirst and urination. Similarly, adverse effects to the anti-convulsants include drowsiness, dizziness, confusion, and nausea. These side-effects usually occur within the initial treatment period – then subside – unless the dosage is too high.

Final Notes

Sometimes when a medication doesn't *appear* effective, it may not be the agent *itself* that's not working, but the *dosage* may merely be miscalculated. What if we knew, for example, via direct communiqué from the Lord Himself that, say, Paxil was the medication of choice for a given kiddo. But, we *under-dose* the child *on* this medication? Well, as a result, we're still *hosed* – falsely assuming the Paxil *itself* was a bust for this particular youngster. In reality, we just didn't have Mark on quite *enough* of this agent.

The neuropsychologic evaluation helps us determine the psychotropic options most likely to work for a given youngster – as well as likely needed dosage ranges – should the parents be open to such. I then work alongside the prescribing physician.

Parenthetically, from my own experience – with rare exceptions – if a youngster is on *four or more* psychotropic medications, we are generally clueless as to the child's correct operational diagnoses – left to blindly search the cold, dark waters of the Corinthian Abyss. It is as if treating clinicians are tossing darts at a dart-board – blind-folded. The *treatment team* does not know what is going on; *you* as parents do not know what is going on; **I** do not know what is going on; *no one* knows what is going on.

> ...with rare exceptions – if a youngster is on four *or more* psychotropic medications, we are generally clueless as to the child's correct operational diagnoses – left to blindly search the cold, dark waters of the Corinthian Abyss.

Consequently, in my experience, *take it to the bank*, that four or more medications – for roughly at least 90% of troubled youth – indicate we do not possess knowledge of the youngster's correct diagnoses. As a result, how can we effectively *treat* a child, or anyone, for that matter, if we don't know what's wrong with them?!

My own bias is to try to keep the vast majority of maltreated youth on no more than *three* psychotropics, *at any one time*. Obviously, there will be exceptions to this guideline. But, by and large, three or less. More than this, and we are treading dangerously on possible polypharmacy.

Summary

Using psychoactive medications with children is an intensely personal decision for parents – which can be quite scary to them. But in certain disorders, a psychotropic makes all the difference in the world. As stated, I see my job as being the very best consultant I can be for the child and parents. Effectively communicating with the parents *all* the various options to help their kiddo – be it medications or *not* – is huge. It is then up to the parents to pray over, and seek out other wise counsel as to what God-led decisions they make to help their youngster.

Chapter 15

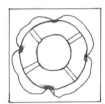

Life Buoys:
Non-Psychopharmacologic Treatment

Medication is not always the best option for treating behavioral health issues. And, there a number of reasons why a parent would chose *not* to have his child on medication: philosophic differences, an adverse reaction to a previous psychotropic trial, an uncooperative youth, etc. And even if a parent decides to *use* a medication for his kiddo, non-psychopharmacologic treatment can further assist most youngsters.

Physical Examination
I often recommend a youth receive a thorough physical exam along with a fairly extensive SMAC series, unless such has already been done within the last 12 months. These are for purposes of ruling out any covert biochemical or endocrine component lurking in the underwater sea-life.

Physical Exercise
Regular bodily exercise has been shown to take some of the bite out of *many* mental health disorders. One of the greatest benefits is

that such improves overall somatic function. But, thoughts/attitudes are rejuvenated, as well.

Exercise can furthermore serve as an outlet for pent-up energy for those struggling with ADHD. Such reduces stress as well as anger. As a person engages in any type of work-out, natural endorphins are released which effect neurotransmitters (brain juices).

In addition, mere sunlight has been proven to be extremely helpful to those struggling with certain forms of depression/mood disorders. SAD (Seasonal Affective Disorder) is a prime example.

> As a person engages in any type of work-out, natural endorphins are released which effect neuro-transmitters (brain juices).

Diet

Food is also a major player in influencing mood. We should ensure, to the best of our ability, that a youth's intake of refined sugar is limited, given the potential disruptive effects of such (e.g., rebound effects after a *sugar high*, etc). Caffeine can disturb the body's natural wake/sleep cycle; so monitoring its intake is important, too, particularly after 5 p.m. Chocolate is an often overlooked source of caffeine that many people fail to take into account. When an adolescent consumes mass quantities of this natural stimulant, it is often a means of self-medicating an underlying mood disorder.

Another dietary issue is food allergies. Such can cause lethargy, skin rashes, diarrhea, mood swings, as well as a long laundry list of other symptoms. For severe food sensitivities, a work-up by a qualified allergist and/or nutritionist is key.

Part of the overall testing procedure may include a strict dietary regimen to determine which specific allergens exist. Keeping a log, with possible connected reactions, is also helpful in tracking down foods a child may be reacting to. Admittedly, raw reality comes into play with this – prohibiting practicality: Dad works outside the home 45 – 50 hours per week, Mom is chauffeur/chief bottle-washer to four kids, with multiple daily *brush fires* breaking out constantly at the absolute most inopportune times. Thus, holding tight to a food log is usually relegated to the **far** stern of the boat.

> When an adolescent consumes mass quantities of [caffeine], it is often a means of self-medicating an underlying mood disorder.

Another known contributor to behavioral mayhem in children is vitamin and mineral deficiencies. With a percentage of youngsters, food sensitivities may produce behavioral mayhem, such as poor attention/concentration, irritability, and – in rare instances – ballistic episodes.

Social Organizations

Most children who have been removed from their family of origin (FOO) wind up with bargain-basement social skills. They have poor peer relations and few friends. These youngsters can benefit from activities which bolster their abilities to relate well with others. Even the simple skill of asking for what one wants is often foreign to these young persons who had to *grab* for anything they ever got.

> Social groups emphasizing interpersonal skills not only improve a child's ability to relate to others, but also enhance self-esteem.

Social groups emphasizing interpersonal skills not only improve a child's ability to relate to others, but also enhance self-esteem.

Clubs of this nature include: Girl Scouts/Boy Scouts, Big Brother/Big Sister programs, Boys and Girls Clubs, Campfire Girls, Optimist Club Football, etc. In addition to developing social *know-how*, these groups often teach leadership skills, provide opportunities to discover new interests and talents, and present challenging situations which cause the youngster to learn resourcefulness. Such also afford opportunities for the sheer joy of accomplishment.

Perhaps the **most** beneficial of all is one's church youth group. Here, we get a *Kuppenheimer's Two-fer Sale*: social skill development *and* spiritual maturity.

Volunteer Organizations

A further option for maltreated youth is volunteering. Volunteer work can do a variety of good: plant the seeds of solid citizenship, enable a kiddo to serve others, as well as enlarge his vision of the world.

Opportunities for volunteering are limited only by one's imagination. In a soup kitchen, a teen learns to serve others – discovering there are many less fortunate than himself. Perhaps he might even learn to appreciate more of what he *has*! Homeless shelters are regularly in need of donations such as blankets, clothing, personal items, etc. An adolescent could sponsor or simply participate in a drive to donate items to such a facility.

> Volunteer work can do a variety of good: plant the seeds of solid citizenship, enable a kiddo to serve others, as well as enlarge his vision of the world.

Nursing homes need people willing to visit those who do not have local family members. Often youth can go on a walk with folks or push an elderly resident's wheelchair on the property grounds. Senior citizens often have many good stories to tell, expanding a teen's horizon beyond herself. An octogenarian, for example, can also add a personal side to history, bringing life to events the kiddo has merely *read about* in textbooks.

An adolescent could also go to the local elementary library after school and help youngsters who are struggling with reading. She could volunteer at a animal kennel, walking the dogs. Or she could regularly, with one or two others, canvas a nearby park, picking up trash. Any and all of these opportunities serve to enhance self-esteem, and contribute to other **people**.

Electroencephalograph Neurofeedback

Another very promising non-pharmacologic treatment for mal-treated youth is EEG Neurofeedback (NFB). Such is showing *very* encouraging results for ADHD, RAD, and mood/anxiety disorders. In addition, EEG Neurofeedback aids overall brain function, sleep patterns, somatic symptoms, conduct problems, drug/alcohol addictions, as well as LDs. Simply stated, this technology teaches people to optimally regulate brain **arousal**.

EEG treatment enables the brain to *retrain* itself via strengthening existing neuro-biologic pathways, as well as learning new ones. EEG work is in many respects analogous to physical exercise. Research indicates that as the resonant

> ...[EEG Neurofeedback] is akin to performing a gradual non-invasive brain surgery, without risk of side effects...

loops within the cortex and sub-cortex are modified (i.e., strengthened or redirected) by EEG NFB, such ensures greater academic learning and decreased neurologic-based disorders. (For research citations pertaining to this exciting modality, go to www.eegspectrum.com.)

The first pioneer of EEG NFB was Dr. Barry Sterman (1974), via his seminal work with seizure disorders. For the last 15 to 20 years, Dr. Joel Lubar (1999) and his associates have been doing excellent research to this clinical application for the treatment of several presenting problems noted above.

Safety and efficacy are two huge pluses for EEG NFB. In essence, this treatment modality is akin to performing a gradual non-invasive brain surgery, without risk of side-effects, when conducted by a well-trained clinician.

As more research is completed, EEG NFB may consistently produce better results than various psychopharmacologic treatments. As I say, further information can be found at www.eegspectrum.com.

Sensory Integration Training

Another new promising approach which appears to greatly help a portion of the maltreated child population is Sensory Integration Therapy (SIT). One of the sequela of early neglect and abuse in a child's life can be Sensory Integration Dysfunction (SID). Such is especially true for internationally adopted kiddoes hailing from, say, an horrific horrific Romanian orphanage. Children con-tinually take in information regarding the environment through their senses. As they receive data, their brain organizes that information and forms a response – be it cogni-tive, be-havioral, etc. If such input for a youngster is lacking, we got trouble in River City – at least temporarily.

If such input for a youngster is lacking, we got trouble in River City – at least temporarily.

In addition to the most frequently cited primary senses – auditory, visual, tactile, olfactory, and gustatory (taste) – there are three additional sensory systems that are very important: tactile, vestibular, and proprioceptive. Sensory integration dysfunction occurs when the brain cannot process the information it receives. It is as if there is a *shipwreck* off the Ivory Coast, by way of sorting out and coordinating information perceived by the various senses.

The tactile system receives information via the skin. The brain processes the sensations of temperature, pressure, pain, etc. If a youngster is struggling with primarily **touch-related** SID, he might exhibit such behaviors as an unwillingness to eat foods of certain textures, experience aversion to tags and/or polyester in clothing, as well as an over- or under-responsiveness to touch.

The vestibular system refers to sensations occurring within the inner ear, enabling us to maintain our balance and equilibrium. If a child is *hypo*sensitive, she may seek out additional stimulation such as rocking, spinning, jumping, etc (*self-stim* behaviors). On the other hand, the *hyper*sensitive child may be fearful of movement which requires balance (i.e., climbing, sliding, swinging).

The proprioceptive system governs the awareness of our body in space. Input also comes into our brain by way of muscles, joints, and ligaments. Hence, the ability to write, draw, or walk up an incline are all part of the proprioceptive system.

Therapy for children with SID is generally conducted by specially trained occupational therapists (OTs). These important clinicians enhance children's sensory messaging systems, allowing them to function more appropriately.

> Additional activities which promote brain integration are: *Follow the Leader, Tag, Simon Says,* tumbling, swinging, and jumping rope.

For the child whose subcortical brain is underdeveloped, SIT focuses on increasing his ability to process sensory cues and messages. Common techniques employed by

SIT clinicians include: practicing balance via sitting on a large rubber ball; improving tactile discrimination through making mud pies or finding small trinkets hidden in clay; enhancing motor coordination by way of running through obstacle courses or playing games with beanbags, balloons, etc.

Additional activities which promote brain integration are: *Follow the Leader*, *Tag*, *Simon Says*, tumbling, swinging, and jumping rope. Furthermore, walking on a balance beam, jumping on a trampoline, playing with large exercise balls are also helpful. For fine-motor skills, finger-paint, squeeze balls, Silly Putty, or nerf ball games can be effective.

Herbal Treatments

Another alternative is herbal treatment – usually related to ADHD symptom neutralization. Simply because I **myself** have not seen efficacy with such does not mean that this form of intervention is necessarily invalid for *all* maltreated youth. A caveat to mention here, herbal treatments **are** medicinal treatments. As such, a physician and/or nutritionist with expertise in this area is needed.

Summary

There are many possible lures for hauling in the big fish. In our tackle box, we need a good supply of spinners, digs, and flies. If the fish aren't biting with the spinner, try the fly. Each child is different and responds uniquely to various options; so we want to keep trying with that kiddo until we discover what works for **him**.

The author's wife and psychometrist, Debbi, checking in Mom
and young teen, Demi, at the beginning of the day's evaluation.

The author conducting a clinical interview with Demi.

Debbi administering a neuropsychologic test to Demi.

The author emerging from the lake, laden down with underwater refuse.

The author (sans his scuba gear!) scoring and analyzing Demi's
neuropsychologic data, in preparation for parent feedback.

The author conducting a 3-hour feedback session on Demi's test
results and recommendations with parents, Tom and Sandi.

The author with wife, Debbi, and son, Forrest.

Chapter 16

Probing Deep Waters: Psychotherapy

With the severity of the youth I see, *conventional* psychotherapy is almost always a bust. Psychologists, along with most mental health professionals, are taught in graduate school that all ills can be successfully treated via *the talking cure*. Such is simply not true. And, I am by no means minimizing the worth of high quality counseling. It is just that *traditional* counseling, and/or Play Therapy, is not the universal panacea our society has made it out to be – for maltreated children and teens. Too many foster kids, for example, are rubber-stamped by state agencies to receive knee-jerk traditional psychotherapy – a huge waste of time and money. But more on that later.

What we **do** need more of are highly trained professionals who can provide Attachment/Bonding Therapy – according to the criteria of ATTACh (Association for the Treatment and Training in the Attachment of Children [**www.attach.org**]). Without an affiliation with this organization, you are short-changing your maltreated youth. The annual conferences **alone** – held in varying parts of the U.S. – are definitely worth the *price of admission*. ATTACh offers much needed hope and direction for parents who are *lost at sea*. Trust me on this.

Attachment/Bonding Therapy

The ability to bond with others is developmentally acquired in infancy. Young babies flourish when there are caring/nurturing adults who respond to their needs and cries. For the children I see, this normal cycle of attachment has been interrupted, usually due to neglect or abuse. The side-effects of such, if left untreated, follow the child into her adolescent and adult years.

Within the area of psychotherapy for maltreated youth, highly trained counselors who specialize in foster/adoptive and attachment issues are sorely needed. I am not talking about the garden-variety/traditionally trained therapist just out of grad school. It is futile to tee-up standard counseling for the vast majority of kiddoes I am discussing in this book. Traditional methods do **not** help these kids! How many tales of frustration and woe have I heard over the years from the parents of maltreated youngsters vis-à-vis having received traditional talk therapy via counselor after counselor after counselor? Answer: **Way** too many to count.

On the other hand, Bonding/Attachment Therapy – along the lines of what a Greg Keck or a Dan Hughes does – *is* what these young persons need. Again, the organization which specializes in this area is ATTACh. Moreover, to once again toss a heavy anchor over the side, if you are a foster or adoptive parent of a maltreated child, and are not an active part of this international organization, you are doing your kiddo a huge disservice.

> …if you are a foster or adoptive parent of a maltreated child, and are not an active part of this international organization, you are doing your kiddo a huge disservice.

The same is true for any **clinician** out there, working with hurt young persons. It is **appalling** how many psychotherapists around the country attempting to help maltreated youth are **not** affiliated with AT-TACh. In fact, many have never even *heard* of this organization. This is greatly distressing to me.

Group Counseling

Group Counseling is an effective, yet oft-ignored, modality for helping troubled teens. Peers have a powerful influence. A caveat here is that group psychotherapy training is a product most of our graduate schools sorely fail to produce – year after year.

The group setting provides a microcosm in which to practice social skills, to work out disagreements, to support and encourage others. A further benefit of meeting with other youth, under direction of a well-trained group counselor, is that the adolescent learns he is not alone in his struggle with aggression/notions of rejection/anxiety, etc.

Group Counseling is actually the *treatment of choice* for young persons beset by Narcissism, Passive-Aggression, Histrionic, and/or Dependent Personality Traits (see Chapter 12). As I say, group counseling dynamics facilitate the learning and practicing of new skills – providing feedback, as well as **genuinely** affirming its members.

> Group Counseling is actually the *treatment of choice* for young persons beset by Narcissism, Passive-Aggression, Histrionic, and/or Dependent Personality Traits.

For adolescents with a character disorder baking in the oven, traditional **individual** talk therapy is toothless. Like trying to *gum* shark meat. However, put these teens in with other like-minded characterologically impaired young people – directed by an experienced, well-trained group therapy clinician – and the gameyness, superficiality, and wholesale manipulation these youth exude can *then* be dealt with.

A superb example of a world-class group psychotherapist is Dr. Ed Furber in Fort Worth, Texas. Dr. Furber, a psychiatrist and esteemed colleague of mine – whose expertise within the group milieu among troubled adolescents was and is unparalleled.

At any rate, aberrant teen behaviors are: (1) quickly recognized by other group members; and (2) confronted – all within the guidance and psychotherapeutic timing brought to the party by a savvy group therapist.

Play Therapy

Young children (ages 4 to 9ish) are not as likely to benefit from individual counseling – of *any* kind – due to their immature language development/thinking skills. These kiddoes simply lack the verbal capabilities to convey their thoughts and feelings – nor the cognitive fire-power needed to effect change. In general, attempting to do non-Play Therapy with children under the age of 10, is a gross exercise in futility.

The purpose of Play Therapy is to allow young people to express their emotions/fears/problems via the non-threatening environment of play. This genre can be helpful for youngsters who have experienced emotional trauma. Hence, kiddoes with PTSD respond very well to Directive Play Therapy. (By way of personal bias, I am **not** a fan of *Non-Directive* Play Therapy for children with moderate to severe RAD – simply turning a kiddo loose in a room of toys and *therapizing* him.)

Bottom line – via play – youngsters are able to symbolically *act out*, rather than discuss, their underlying psychologic currents. By interacting with and observing the child, a well-trained directive play therapist can glean information which the kiddo could *never* in a millennium convey **verbally**. Counselors use a variety of forums here: games, dolls, puppets, drawing, role-playing, water-colors, etc.

Especially with **young** kiddoes, educating their adult caregivers/teachers is crucially important. Parents can reinforce – in tandem with Directive Play Therapy – healthy responses for the child.

Common *horse-sense* dictates that parent figures possess the largest probability for helping troubled kiddos. After all, they are **with** these children for the majority of each week (excepting perhaps protracted day-care situations).

Biochemical Considerations

An important footnote, as cited before, is that *any form* of counseling will not avail much – if anything – for the youth with a Borderline Condition, until she is stabilized on the appropriate medication(s). Even the most preeminent of psychotherapists will not be able to substantially impact a child/teen within the throes of a subtle thought disorder and/or mild perceptual distortion. Attempting to render counseling with a youngster who possesses a BC is exasperating to everyone involved: the therapist, parent, *and* kiddo. (Such probably doesn't do a great deal for God either.) However, once the appropriate psychotropic *kicks-in* for the BC, progress often occurs, and occurs quickly.

Family Therapy

This form of therapy is frequently used in conjunction with effective Individual Counseling. The primary reason is that families are dynamic/ever-changing systems. Each individual part effects the whole. Therefore, when one member of the family system begins to behave in new ways, all other members must correspondingly adjust. While the changes

> Family Therapy is frequently used in conjunction with effective Individual Counseling.

may be for the common good – via both the individual *and* her family – the *system* must reestablish a different **equilibrium**. New patterns of relating must be found. Consequently, periodic Family Therapy is often hugely important for a maltreated youth.

Eye Movement Desensitization and Reprocessing

Eye Movement Desensitization and Reprocessing (EMDR) is a psychotherapy technique most commonly used with young persons suffering from Post-traumatic Stress Disorder (Shapiro, 1989). PTSD often involves depression, anxiety, recurrent nightmares, panic episodes, and phobias – all of which EMDR can help address – most frequently with kiddoes suffering from neglect, abuse, or other distressing experiences.

EMDR is a noninvasive therapy which aids a young person in working through a traumatic event. When such occurs, the thoughts, emotions, sights, and sounds of that experience are imprinted upon the brain. Because a youngster does not know **how** to process the trauma he has experienced, the aversive feelings tend to remain **with** the child.

> EMDR is a noninvasive therapy which aids a young person in working through a traumatic event.

EMDR is designed to help a youngster process and move beyond these *stuck* feelings. The therapy resurfaces the distressing situation, along with the accompanying emotions, but then allows the youth to *reprocess* them. The result is that a youngster can subsequently remember the event, but the toxic emotions are no longer as debilitating.

Personally, from what I have seen – in conjunction with research (Greenwald, 1999; Lovett, 1999) – EMDR can in fact play a helpful role within the treatment arsenal for neglected and abused young persons. Case reports conclude that this treatment modality is not only effective, but may even produce faster results for **children**, as opposed to adults (Cocco & Sharpe, 1993).

Perhaps the single most unfortunate aspect of EMDR is the *name* that was initially chosen for it. Even Shapiro herself, I am told, opines that this form of treatment would have been better served by labeling it something akin to "Brain Reprocessing Therapy." Finally, it goes without saying EMDR should be performed by specially trained counselors.

Equine/Pet Therapy

Another treatment option is Equine Assisted Therapy. Such is designed to improve a young person's overall emotional/behavioral status via interaction with horses and/or other animals. These programs are designed to enhance people-skills such as bonding, teamwork, and cooperation. Furthermore – especially via Equine Therapy – there are many benefits on the individual level: improving muscle strength, balance and coordination, facilitating speech and language development, building empathy, and increasing self-esteem. A superb equine clinician, who also possesses impeccable Bonding/Attachment Therapy skills, is Kathy Baczynski, MS, LPC, in Weatherford, Texas. Like unto Dr. Furber within the sphere of adolescent group psychotherapy, Kathy is the real deal.

Equine work proves beneficial for autism, conduct disorders, PTSD, depression, RAD, ADHD, as well as a host of other childhood disorders. There are programs available in most areas. It is worth checking into.

In fact, most animals we tend to have as pets can be great therapeutic agents. Dogs, in particular, provide

> ...petting an animal actually *lowers blood pressure,* and helps relieve depression!

155

youth with unconditional love. For most people, petting an animal actually *lowers blood pressure*, and helps relieve depression!

Some teens, who do not feel comfortable talking to people, *will* talk to non-humans. Why might this be? Simply because the animal *listens* wholeheartedly, fully accepting the words/emotions (if I may anthropomorphize a bit here) which come bubbling up from the bowels of a youth's cargo ship.

Pets can also foster responsibility in a child – by requiring the young person to feed, exercise, and play with her pet. Moreover, in having charge over the little creature, the youngster begins to think about **another's** welfare, other than just her own.

Summary

The bottom line is that unless we clean up certain kinds of deep sea refuse for young persons (a Borderline Condition, for example), *any* kind of psychotherapy will be of minimal help. This I have seen over and over – *ad nauseam* – via 22 years of clinical practice. Said another way, it's impossible to catch healthy fish from a toxic-dump reservoir. First, we have to clean out the lake. Then, Bonding/Attachment Therapy via a trained clinician, preferably affiliated with ATTACh, is crucial.

Traditional counseling with the vast majority of maltreated youth is a waste of good time and money. Unfortunately, most state child welfare agencies don't require proper therapist credentialing, **vis-à-vis** **Bonding/Attachment Therapy**. To do otherwise – especially with a case of RAD – is tantamount to enlisting a family practitioner to perform brain surgery.

It's up to you, the parent, to ensure **your** kiddo receives the appropriate help from a well-trained attachment clinician.

Chapter 17

A Lighthouse!: Increasing Academic Motivation

Academic underachievement is, I am convinced, the curse of too many red-blooded young American males. Sure, there have always been kids – down through the years – who sloughed off their work, perpetually playing hooky down at the local fishing hole. Yet now, academic underachievement seems to be of epidemic proportions.

> For this kiddo, the more parents and teachers do *for* him, the less he does for *himself.*

A Dependent Underachiever (DU) is defined as a youngster who is not performing up to his capability within the academic arena (sound like anyone **you** know??).

For this kiddo, the more parents and teachers do *for* him, the less he does for *himself.* If you think about it, this is common sense. The more **we** do for him, the more dependent **he** becomes. So our primary goal for a DU is to increase *his* effort in matters related to school. Increasing **effort** increases independence.

By the way, much of my own approach to helping Dependent Underachievers get the sand out of their swim-trunks has been shaped by Dr. Sylvia Rimm (Rimm, 1995), a former teacher turned psychologist – the nation's foremost authority on rescuing DUs once they fall overboard.

One caveat here: among RAD youth, only a portion of what I will be talking about in this chapter will apply.

"Gettin' By"

My father, Ed Gray, came from a rural family who settled in the fertile blackland of northeast Texas, near Greenville. He was the youngest of five siblings – three of whom were sisters – all subsequently becoming teachers. One of them, my Aunt Allene, earned a master's degree in Latin from the University of Texas at Austin. She became a world-class high school teacher for approximately 78 years, at my alma mater, Cleburne High School – Home of the *Fighting Yellow Jackets*. So, growing up, my dear old dad was no stranger to a family environment rife with academic excellence.

Nevertheless, I recall asking him several times over the years (I suppose I wondered if his answer would ever **change** – which it never did), "Pop, what kind of grades did *you* make in school?"

His verbatim answer on each and every occasion was, "I got *by*."

Despite a less than auspicious academic career, my dad was a bright man who went on to do well in business as a haberdasher, armed with a high school diploma – never having done more in school than "*gettin' by*." He owned and operated Gray's Men's Wear on the south side of the market square in Cleburne, Texas for over 20 years.

Helping the Underachiever: Routines

There are ways to help students who do even *less* than "*gettin' by*." The first of which is routines. Structure is *vital* to the Dependent Underachiever while we try to get him turned around. A routine helps to increase independence. An established *modus operandus* takes the chaos out of mornings – not to mention the beef-up of academic responsibility/homework completion, as well as chores.

Goal Setting

Goal setting is another all-important skill for DUs to learn. Regular study time is a must in helping them set and meet goals. If we are working with Mark on his weekly spelling list, a goal for the session might be to correctly spell – to dictation – eight out of ten words. After he studies, we give him a trial run-through of the ten words.

> Structure is *vital* to the Dependent Underachiever while we try to get him turned around.

If Mark *meets* the goal, he is then released from custody, to pursue his own free-time. He has ***earrrrrned*** it. On the other hand, should he correctly spell only six out of the ten words, then it is back to the list, for 15 more minutes of study. Then we test him again, repeating the process until he reaches at least the 80% hit-rate. So not only is Mark learning his spelling words, but he is acquiring the vital skills of giving **effort**, along with setting goals.

> No siblings should interrupt homework time, under threat of exile to a Siberian work-camp.

A Place for Study

To facilitate autonomous study habits, provide the youth with a new desk. Or perhaps we only need do the ceremonial purging – uncovering the desk that Heather already possesses, buried somewhere within the dark recesses of her room. We bought the desk for her 6 years ago, and we are certain it's still in there –

somewhere.

Anyway, this unveiling sets the stage for new independence. Cleanse the workstation. The desk or table should typically be in a separate room, away from family traffic. No siblings should interrupt homework time, under threat of exile to a Siberian work-camp. Obviously, TV should be off-limits in the initial stages of establishing the youth's new autonomy. The one exception I have found is that *some* young persons **do** study better by virtue of listening to low decibels of classical music, for example. That is **fine**.

Implementing the Independent Plan

Our goal for the DU is Mark *himself* taking over responsibility for his scholastic endeavors. This is done gradually, over time. A youngster needs *encouragement* in moving toward this goal. It is up to us though to appropriately help him.

First, I sit down with you as parents, and we develop an independent homework plan, much as a scuba person determines his dive route. We construct a homework routine that works for *your* family and *your* schedule. We also develop a reward system to enhance your child's *MO* (motivation) level.

Equipped with our blueprint, we bring Mark in to discuss the *dive plan*. I lead off with the announcement of an increased allowance (previously agreed to by the parents, of course). Remarkably, I have never had a child or teen refuse this offer! Then, I turn the discussion to the newly delineated academic goals – such as getting homework done every day, avoiding zeroes, and the like. I tell Mark that with the accomplishment of these goals, special privileges can be earned.

At this point, I explain the homework *Assignment Sheet* (see Figure 17.1). I conclude this part of the discussion by emphasizing to the youth that *he* is responsible for writing the assignments on the sheet, and that such needs to be **legible**. Included in this discussion are the new homework routine, and place of study.

Then, I move onto the potential rewards. Goodies that can be earned need to be defined at the beginning of the new regimen. Short-term carrots that can be earned (on a daily basis) might be, for example: TV privileges, Nintendo access, outside free-time, playing a board game with a parent, etc.

Boys love *man-to-man* time with their dads. One of the most powerful reinforcers for young males is to have **time** with Dad: shooting hoops, working on the car, playing a computer game, etc.

There are also *long-term* privileges that can be earned. Suppose Mark goes a full week, gets all homework turned in, with no evidence from a teacher that any zeroes have come through the wash. The youngster has thus, for example, successfully met his goals for the entire week. In response to this happy event, a weekend movie or bowling with Dad might be some things he could earn. Other ideas are a weekend fishing trip, pizza party with two friends, a best bud to sleep over on Friday night, etc. And just as guys relish man-to-man time with Dad via sports, etc, many girls love to shop at the mall, *or* play sports with *Mom*.

> Goodies that can be earned need to be defined at the beginning of the new regimen.

Additionally, we should set even *longer* range goals. If Mark turns in all work for a 4-week period, for example, his success might be rewarded with a night-time baseball game, trip to an amusement park, etc. Each family can creatively mold and shape the various carrots that fit their budget, and the child's interests.

When the youth has tangible goals that mean something to **him**, in most cases he develops the motivation within himself to turn around the vexing academic underachievement. Think about it – how hard would *you* work at your job if your paycheck came on only a hit-

or-miss basis? How motivated would **you** be? But, the kind of motivation metamorphosis we're talking about takes time – weeks to *months*.

Teacher-Parent Conduit

The teacher-parent conduit is another vital piece of the puzzle. Most teachers are more than willing to cooperate in order to help a youngster become responsible for handling his own school work. So the first step is conferring with the teacher to see if he/she is willing to participate.

Figure 17.1 is an example of a weekly homework sheet you might want to use. Mine is no better or worse than anyone else's, but it's a starting place. Heather is responsible for filling in the homework assignment on each subject for that particular evening. For example, for math homework, she writes *problems one through ten, page 38* in the appropriate box (see Figure 17.1).

> Heather shows the Homework Assignment Sheet to the teacher at the end of the class...

Heather shows her Assignment Sheet to the teacher at the end of the class – with the appropriate homework, filled in *by* Heather. The instructor merely initials the entry. So, we are really not asking the teacher to do a whole lot; simply look at and initial the paper. Then under the *Comments* column, the teacher can write any cogent messages to the parents, such as an MIA assignment for that day, etc. A code of sorts, can also be worked out – a little insignia, for example – so the parent knows there is a zero that occurred, or what have you. Parents who ask teachers to help should let them know how much this extra effort on their part is appreciated.

Attaching both positive and adverse consequences to the task of bringing home the assignment sheet is needed. The consequences should not be large. But they *should* be daily. One of the most effec-

162

tive rewards for delivering the assignment sheet is 15 minutes of father/son or mother/daughter alone-time each night. But, this can be anything feasible that the youth prizes.

I personally like the use of small monetary sums as rewards – should money *be* a reinforcer for a child. Some parents are uncomfortable with such, and I respect this. However, our role *as parents* is to gradually prepare youngsters for adulthood. As adults, we work for *money*. So why not have **kids** work for money also (albeit in much smaller amounts).

Homework Assignment Sheet

	Monday	Tuesday	Wednesday	Thursday	Friday	Comments
Reading						
Spelling						
Math						
Social Studies						
Science						
Art						

Figure 17.1   Homework Assignment Sheet

An even better system of parent-teacher communication entails having the youth's class homework assignments available on-line – accessible directly *to* the parents on, say, each Monday of the week by way of a website. An excellent example of this is conducted by Lewis-Palmer School District 38 in Monument, Colorado (www.lpsd.co.us). Other school districts have similar on-line data listed on **their** web pages, easily within reach of any parent with a PC.

Adverse consequences should be employed were Heather to *not* bring her assignment sheet from school. For example, a loss of TV time or outside play time – for that day/evening – will keep the homework sheets coming.

My experience is that once this system is started, a youngster will test us in the early going – the first week or two – with one or more *end-runs*. So, we should just expect she is initially going to lose a couple of assignment sheets off the starboard side. The child is basically asking if said consequences will be enforced. If the *bugaboo* for this form going MIA is *grounding* for that night (specifically: no TV/Nintendo), are we going to follow through with it?

Teacher/parent consistency is crucial. This means that despite busy after-school schedules, parents **must** review the communications faithfully and encourage progress. Too many cues and reminders from parents and/or teachers, however, cause *more* dependence. It is better

> My experience is that once an assignment sheet is started, a youngster will test us in the early going – the first week or two, with one or more *end-runs*.

to simply enforce the consequences until the child performs, rather than giving never-ending cues and reminders by way of verbal diarrhea.

Problem Areas: "Mom, I Don't *Understand* This Stuff!"

How many times have you heard your kiddo say, "Mom, I don't understand this stuff *^#>•✗⊕◄...!" Before immediately doling out help, ask yourself, "Does my child honestly not *understand* the work, or is this merely wanton manipulation?" As parents, we often do not allow our children to struggle a bit with tasks that are difficult, or that require *effort*. But we **need** to. Tell the youngster to try to understand it on his own before coming for help.

After attempting it on his own and then soliciting help, ask, "Well, Mark, tell me what you *do* understand here." Start with teasing out of him what he *does* know. Then slowly describe the concept and permit your youth to try one homework item in your immediate presence. Then insist that he go back to his workstation to finish the rest (Rimm, 1995).

Whenever possible, the father should be in charge of monitoring the homework for boys – or at least *involved* with such. Mom might need to look over it at the end of the homework period, when Dad is not home from work yet, but getting Dad into the loop, at least briefly during the evening, is very powerful for boys. Interested and persistent fathers are extremely effective in communicating a serious school work message to DU *boys*.

> ...getting Dad into the loop, at least briefly during the evening, is very powerful for boys.

Setting Realistic Expectations

We need to have appropriate expectations for our youth, via the typical human learning curve. One of our jobs is helping Heather learn how to deal constructively with failure. She should view each small defeat as a learning experience, to determine the extent of effort necessary to reach her goals. If we over-react as parents, we only confirm Heather's suspicions that she cannot really be successful **after all**.

Studies done both on animals and humans show a common phenomenon when it comes to learning a new task (in this case, a child taking charge of her academic work and learning good study habits).

Typically, we'll see a youngster make initial progress toward mastering new skills. But then come dips and downturns along the way; subsequently, it is three steps forward and one step back; two steps forward, one step back; four steps forward, two steps back. There **will** be a *jagged* learning curve, but one that shows overall improvement – nevertheless, with inevitable setbacks along the way.

Moreover, there is the cryptic *Ah-ha Experience*. Here, after months or perhaps **years** of the *three steps forward – one step back* routine, a light bulb seems to abruptly switch on for a kiddo. This is the *Ah-ha Experience*, wherein Heather finally grasps what her parents have been trying to teach her since 2nd grade. Namely, that she indeed **can** be and **is** an Independent Achiever. Praise **God**!

> There **will** be a *jagged* learning curve, but one that shows over-all improvement – nevertheless, with inevitable setbacks along the way.

Wish List

The Wish List for young DUs, if they would be honest with us (which they **won't** be), are:

(1) Help me become a better creative problem solver – that is, give the problem back to me, or ask *me* to think about it for an hour or so before I can get your help; and

(2) Assist *me* in being accountable for my efforts – withhold your attention from me until I make the *effort* (Cornale, 1993).

Now, human nature being what it is for us as parents, when do we typically give our *attention*? Right, when there are problems. What these kiddoes need is to learn to work problems out for themselves, with our guidance in doing so. It's our job as parents, to **teach** them this process.

Summary

We can help our children become better students by placing the onus on *them* to perform up *to* the level of their academic ability. Youth will let teachers and parents do the work **for** them as long as youngsters can get away with it. Routines and goals, along with concrete motivational aides, are crucial in transforming a Dependent Underachiever to Independent Achiever status!

Chapter 18

All Hands on Deck!: School Options

Doing well in the classroom for a young person is a big deal. As adults, we all have jobs – either inside or outside the home. Oft-times **both**. School is a youth's *job*. Hence, if events within the *workplace* are rotten, how will this influence a kiddo's self-esteem, not to mention peace at home? You catch my drift.

The other vital consideration here, of course, is that school performance often sets the tone for *later* options – vocational life in particular. How many times have we encountered an otherwise bright and capable youth **not** attend college, or fail to engage an occupation that would on the surface at least appear to be a tight fit for him? Exactly. More often than we like to see.

> The key here though is *calling* – specifically, *God's* calling.

Not, mind you, that there is anything at all wrong with so-called *blue-collar* jobs. How arrogant would we be to suggest there is dishonor in an occupation not requiring a high school diploma. The key here though is *calling* – specifically, *God's* calling. If

God has called me to negotiate a sanitation truck, so be it. And hopefully, I will operate that vehicle with competence, and as a witness for Christ. Likewise, if He has called me to become a neurosurgeon, may I *also* operate with skill (no pun intended) – **and** as a witness for Christ.

The real issue, then, is God-endowed vocation. The term itself hails from the Latin *vocare – to call*. (Yes, I **did** learn a bit of Latin in high school/college – much to the delight of my dear deceased aunt, Allene Gray, who taught this ancient language at my hometown high school – prior to her retirement in the late 60s.)

At any rate, our charge as parents is to help equip our sons and daughters obtain the wherewithal to be as successful in school as God would have them to be. Why? So they do not needlessly paint themselves into a corner, precluding later higher education which in turn could ultimately obstruct the vocation God has prescribed **for** them.

> ...we help our children become the best students they can be...

So, as we help our children become the best students they can be, what options are available to aid their academic success?

Modified Curricula

Modified Curricula is an adjustment in the **content** of education, rather than the setting. Here, a student stays in the Regular Ed classroom but is responsible for less material (e.g., fifteen spelling words vs. twenty; ten math problems vs. fifteen; one chapter to read vs. two, etc). Moreover, a student might be in Resource (discussed below) for Language Arts and Math, while receiving Modified Curricula for everything else.

Content Mastery

Content Mastery (CM) is provided in most Texas school districts. Many other states have something similar. CM is available to Regular Ed students who do not qualify for Special Ed, but who nevertheless are struggling in a particular academic subject. Such can specifically target a child's *Achilles' Heel*, revealed by any of several tests of academic skills. Think of this as individual/small group tutoring, held in a separate room within the school.

CM usually consists of a teacher, or aide, and anywhere from two to ten students. It can vary in frequency from daily to PRN (as needed) assistance. A youngster may receive help in one, two, or more classes – depending upon the needs of the child. Language Arts, for example, is frequently an area targeted by CM.

Resource

Resource is a special classroom environment generally designed for students coded LD. Such usually consists of a teacher, an aide, and fifteen or less students. Youth who qualify might attend Resource for one, two, or **more** daily subjects. Here, teachers present modified material to students who are not able to pursue a more rigorous curricula.

Self-Contained Classroom

At times a child may carry a Special Ed coding of Emotionally Disturbed (ED). Such is appropriate when the youngster suffers from a mental disorder such as Dysthymic Disorder of Childhood, a Borderline Condition, etc. Oppositionalism, verbal aggression, and/or tantrums may be frequent. In light of such, the youth is assigned to a Self-Contained classroom consisting of a teacher and an aide – along with approximately six to eight students.

Transitional Classroom

This is much like a Self-Contained classroom, by way of utilization of a behavior modification system, a high teacher-student ratio, etc. The difference: it's of short-term duration – usually only 6 to 8 weeks. After that, the student is *transitioned* back to his home campus or Regular Ed classroom.

Developmental Skills Classroom

Developmental Skills are classes which help Mentally Retarded (MR) youth within the arenas of self-care, receptive/expressive language, independent living skills, social/emotional skills, academics, and economic self-sufficiency. Moreover, these classes can be tailored to an individual student's needs.

Speech Therapy

A child who struggles with a pronounced language and/or articulation disorder has access to speech therapy from the school system. (The coding, at least in Texas, is *Speech Impaired* – or SI.) This is conducted by a licensed Speech Pathologist. By the way, a good Speech Pathologist is worth her weight in gold.

Other Health Impaired

An OHI classification can be due to: a serious heart condition, a pronounced ADHD, cancer, paraplegia, a head injury, etc. Depending on the severity and impairment of a child's disorder, the student may be placed in an altogether separate classroom (such as Developmental Skills, if also MR), Resource – or simply receive a Tex-Mex Combo Plate of, for example, Modified Curricula, Speech Therapy, plus CM.

Individualized Education Plan (IEP)

Since the 1970s, all schools have been required by law to offer Individual-

> Since the 1970s, all schools have been required by law to offer Individualized Education Plans (IEPs) for Special Education students.

ized Education Plans (IEPs) for Special Education students. IEPs include the current academic performance of the child, educational goals for the year, specific services which are required, timelines for obtainment of said goals, delineation of responsibilities among school staff (i.e., who on campus is supposed to do *what*), as well as objective evaluation procedures.

Admission, Review, and Dismissal

An ARD (Admission, Review, and Dismissal) committee is set up at a student's school to determine if a child needs Special Ed services. If the committee determines the youngster qualifies for this type of additional assistance, then the group writes up an IEP. The ARD committee also reviews IEP goals and objectives on an annual basis – as well as a *full-bore* evaluation of the youngster every 3 years (a 3-Year Re-eval). In addition, the group is responsible to procure the least restrictive educational environment for the kiddo.

The ARD committee is generally made up of...parents, teachers,... the student (if appropriate), educational diagnostician, school psychologist, as well as any other applicable professional personnel...

The ARD committee is generally made up of the following people: parents, teachers (Regular and Special Ed), the student (if appropriate), educational diagnostician, school psychologist, as well as any other applicable professional personnel as needed (school nurse, instructor for the deaf, etc).

Tutoring

Many students benefit from good quality professional tutoring – beyond that which a school district can provide. Again, I often see a *big-time* need to target Language Arts skills: (1) phonics; (2) spelling/ sight-word vocabulary; (3) punctuation/capitalization rules; (4) verb/ noun usage; and (5) compositional writing.

Generally, school districts have a list of tutors which you can call, should the school *itself* not possess quality tutorial options. Networking with other parents can also provide assistance regarding the best tutors in your area.

A prime example – in Colorado Springs where I live – is Ms. Nan Koehler. Nan is without question the most effective personal tutor I have ever met. (Nan, where were you during my sophomore year of high school geometry?) Another option would be a national chain such as *The Sylvan Learning Centers* (1-800-Educate).

> ...I often see a *big-time* need to target Language Arts skills...

An accompanying *Motivation Plan* is often helpful for ensuring that the parents' investment in tutoring is not for naught. A *Motivation Plan* links the youngster's **attitude** and **participation** in said sessions with tangible rewards (see Chapter 17).

Gifted & Talented

Other students benefit from placement into the Gifted and Talented (G&T) program at their respective schools. For example, *some* behavioral problems in the classroom can be traced to unmitigated boredom, wherein a 7 year-old child must sit through a 2nd grade reading lesson, even though his reading skills are on a 6th grade level.

Special Education Advocacy

The Individuals with Disabilities Education Act (IDEA) requires states to sufficiently educate any child with a disability. Youngsters between the ages of birth to 5 with special needs are also eligible for various services. Qualification for such accommodations is determined via an evaluation done by the local school district – or by an outside consultant. I myself have performed many of these examinations throughout 20 years of private practice.

Furthermore, The Rehabilitation Act of 1973 – Section 504 – ensures that schools must provide reasonable accommodations for students who have trouble with one or more *major life activities*. Examples of such are: walking, breathing, seeing, hearing, speaking, caring for oneself, performing manual tasks, etc.

Another available resource in each region is the Parent Training and Information Center (PTIC). This organization can help moms and dads negotiate the policies and procedures of their state to ensure the best/most appropriate education for their child. The PTIC web address is www.pacer.org. The appropriate contact persons are listed. Not only can this agency help guide a parent through the convoluted maze of Special Ed, PTIC publishes a newsletter, as well as offers many educational materials.

> Another available resource in each region is the Parent Training and Information Center (PTIC). This organization can help moms and dads negotiate the policies and procedures of their state to ensure the best/most appropriate education for their child.

Should there be questions regarding their young person's rights within the classroom, I would refer them to the Special Education Department of their own school district. Moreover, in Texas – for example – Advocacy, Incorporated (1-800-880-2884) exists to assist parents who are frustrated in dealing with their youth's school, by helping them obtain Special Ed services, if appropriate. A representative from such a group can even attend an ARD meeting with the parents, should such be needed or desired. In every part of the U.S., non-profit education-advocacy groups exist.

Summary

Maltreated youth come in all shapes and sizes, with a varied assortment of underwater refuse. One of our responsibilities as a parent is to advocate for the appropriate educational needs of our kids. Remember, true vocation is a *calling*. Appropriate education is a precursor to a youth's ability to fulfill God's plan for his life.

Chapter 19

Taming the Sharks:
Behavioral Strategies

As a result of my own years in the trenches, it is obvious that parents need a seafood smorgasbord of behavioral strategies when dealing with maltreated youth. It however goes without saying that not every technique works for every child. But usually, at least *something* works for any given youngster – if we stay diligent and not allow ourselves to get frazzled. It also helps to guard against parental rigidity ("I *tried* time-out – it didn't *work!*").

Toxic Verbal Gameyness

Parents, take **heart**! It *is* possible to significantly reduce the amount of verbiage employed in dealing with a youth and in setting limits for him, diffusing what I term *TVG – Toxic Verbal Gameyness* (Gray, 1999). As we know, many a Choleric/Narcissistic youngster is all too quick to argue and debate with authority figures.

But, it takes *two to Tango* in Tangiers, and there is nobody ramming bamboo shoots up our fingernails – shouting, **"Debate!"** Not only is TVG tremendously draining for us as parents, but such also constitutes a subtle means of enhancing Heather's inappropriate power base within the home.

Unfortunately, in our society we over-value talking, explaining, pontificating, debating, *ad infinitum,* to our children as we lovingly mete out discipline to them. I have found that this tack typically does **not** work. Moreover, such is usually **counterproductive**.

If Heather is constantly arguing within the home, it speaks to the notion that she has established *gamesmanship*. Hence, we must place a United Nations boycott on *return fire* with the lass. *She* can certainly rant and rave, to her heart's content. However, as I say, it takes at least two persons to *argue*.

> ...in our society we over-value talking, explaining, pontificating, debating, *ad infinitum,* to our children as we lovingly mete out discipline to them.

Thus, parents simply have to gently, but firmly, lay down the law to the youth that from now on they will no longer be playing *Debate Club* with her.

Of course, the real art form with this approach is our ability to communicate such in a matter-of-fact/low-key manner – adding in a dash of subtle jocularity, as in, "Oh, Heather, remember? I was kicked **off** Debate Team in high school. I'm really **lousy** at it..."

Anti-arguing Instructions

Below are some tips that work well to short-circuit the nagging youth so often pursue with us (Rimm, 1995). When arguers come at you, remind yourself **not** to say yes **or** no immediately. Instead, after Heather has made a request: (1) ask for her reasons. In requesting such, she can never accuse you of not **listening**.

After **hearing** her reasons, (2) say: "Let me think about it. I'll get back to you..." For a small petition from Heather, take a few minutes or wait until after dinner before giving your reply. Delay the response until tomorrow or the weekend, for a larger request (Rimm, 1995).

There are three marvelous benefits to #2. First, it allows you to be **rational**. Secondly, it teaches children to be patient. Many mal-treated youngsters demand instant gratification; so forbearance is a good quality for them to learn – another component of healthy pre-frontal lobes. Thirdly, given that an arguer knows you have not yet responded with either a yes **or** a no, she realizes that being *good* increases the likelihood of receiving a favorable answer later on. Kind of sneaky, no?...I don't **care**.

Then think about her request and the reasons. Do not be adversely biased by your feelings or any pushiness on **her** part. If the answer is yes, smile and say so. Be upbeat. Choleric/Narcissistic youngsters rarely see adults smile. If the decision is a compromise, explain such enthusiastically. If your answer is no – and parents do have the right and obligation to refuse – even if it is only because you are too tired to drive her someplace – then *say* no calmly and firmly (Rimm, 1995).

Include your reasoning as part of the refusal. Rimm recommends keeping to your original decision approximately 90% of the time. You may *rethink* your choice 10% or so of the time, for flexibility's sake. After all, rigidity rarely has a place in child-rearing. But do not engage in further discussion. Do not let Heather make you feel guilty (*guilt-jerking*). Of course, Choleric/Narcissistic/RAD youth are past-masters at this. It is a prime form of their manipulation. "If I can get Mom to feel bad enough, she'll *cave...*"

> If Heather is too big to time out, you calmly go to **your** room and lock the door.

So, to re-cap: (1) hear her request – listen to her reasons; (2) think about them carefully; and then – after a time – (3) give her your answer, **as well as** the rationale. The discussion is now done. *Finito. Kaput. Sayanara. Auf Wiedersehn.* **Bye**-bye.

If she *continues* arguing, and is below age 10 and not too big, send her little bottom to time-out. If Heather is too big to time out, you calmly go to **your** room and lock the door. (See Time-Out for Teens, later in this chapter.) If she beats on your door – or otherwise spits, curses, fumes, sprays out noxious mucosal refuse – **ignore** it. Relax with a good book or turn on the TV. Eventually, most kiddoes learn that parents have the privilege of saying no (Rimm, 1995).

Audio Therapy

Another handy way to counter snotty verbiage and/or tantrums is Audio Therapy (Gray, 2000). This approach entails utilization of a small/inexpensive micro-cassette recorder to capture episodes of verbal sassing/*smart-mouth* rampagings from your youth. Then, such can be immediately, or later on, played back for all to hear. It is again very important that this is done in an off-handed, almost playful fashion by the parent. ("Whoops! Let's hear that sound-bite **again**, Mark.")

VideoCam Therapy

Similar to the above, VideoCam Therapy (Gray, 2000) targets ballistic episodes. This strategy entails informing Heather that we will, from now on, need to *film* her tantrums for use in the upcoming horror sequel, *An American Werewolf in Pittsburgh*, by Steven Spielberg, starring Billy Bob Thornton and Kathy Bates – with a brief cameo appearance by the Rev. Al Sharpton. Then, keep your trusty camcorder handy, taping a piece of her explosions.

> ...keep your trusty camcorder handy, taping a piece of her explosions.

Once a video clip is made, the excerpt can later on – at a parent's convenience – be watched, while concurrently providing a tongue-in-cheek John Madden running commentary on what the youth is doing *on* the tape. Heather should be at home during the time (or **times**) of viewing, but not coerced into watching it. However, most kiddoes' curiosity gets the best of them here! Many youngsters have never before considered what their tantrums *actually look and sound like*, and are jolted by seeing their mayhem in resplendent technicolor.

Squirt-Gun Therapy

Another *tantrum technique* is Squirt-Gun Therapy (Gray, 2000). Here, a parent informs Mark that, in an attempt to avoid punctured eardrums during loud sessions of wayward vocalizations, we will henceforth be giving brief/random squirts to the mouth during tantrums. Then, on occasions when Mark raises his volume to that of a *Kiss* concert, calmly take aim at his mouth and squeeze off a few. Again, playful jocularity here is key. (Note: states' foster care edicts frown upon Squirt-Gun Therapy for foster kids. However, this technique is no problem for adoptive or biologic youth.)

PlugHugger Device

I also recommend the PlugHugger device (Rimm, 1995). This little gizmo can be used so as to grease the wheel by way of limiting a child's access to electronic devices of pleasure – *Nintendo*, TV, jambox, etc – during periods of restriction.

The PlugHugger slides easily onto the AC for most electronic equipment, thus rendering such temporarily *kaput*. The devise can only be taken off by a metal key which is safely in your keeping. A phone number to obtain this little gem is 1-800-475-1118 (Educational Assessments Services, Inc). Or you can call Home Depot at 1-800-430-3376.

Bland Sandwich Therapy

In terms of another behavioral approach, parents should consider *Bland Sandwich Therapy* (Gray and Blue, 1999). Here, a child who is in need of attitude adjustment is required – again, on days of restricted privileges – to eat a sandwich brought from home, as opposed to choosing an item from the menu, should the family be dining out at a fast-food joint, or doing carry-out from the local pizza parlor for dinner.

My particular *Ye Olde Bland Sandwich Special* is a slice of tomato and some lettuce, with a dab of mustard. (For Epicurean youth, *Grey Poupon* can suffice.) Or, the traditional peanut butter and jelly will do. But the sandwich, whatever its contents, should be bland – **not** obtained from *Jason's Deli* (!).

Time-Out

This technique has received a bad rap, often soundly *pooh-poohed* by parents. To be sure, there is no question that with moderate to severe RAD youth, time-out simply does not **work** – even when executed to perfection. Yet this procedure *can* be extremely effective with many youngsters, **if** administered correctly. On the other hand, I have also seen the improper implementation of this technique not only *fail*, but frequently make a child's behavior *worse*. **Yikes**.

Time-out should occur only for predetermined offenses which have been explained to Mark ahead of time. Immediately following a transgression, the youth should be directed to the time-out locale – calmly and with minimal verbiage – devoid of shouting or teeth-gnashing by us. If the time requirement is 10 minutes, then the time starts once he is *on location* **and** quiet. *Once the sentence has been served, no further discussion, haranguing, de-briefing **or** explaining should occur afterward by the parent.*

After a few trips to time-out, a **warning** is frequently all that is needed to straighten out many youngsters. Make sure you do not deliver more than one warning. Then, make sure to follow through if the behavior does not stop.

An important side-bar here is that time-outs for Mark should **not** take place in his own room, wherein lie favorite games and toys. Such becomes tantamount to rewarding rotten behavior. Rather, time-out should be served up within a sterile setting – the blandest of the bland – wherein the youngster cannot see what is going on in the family.

Parents seeking additional information on this technique should sneak a peek at Dr. Sylvia Rimm's "Recipe for Successful Time-Outs" from her book, *Why Bright Kids Get Poor Grades* (1995). Dr. Rimm includes some of the common mistakes that **ensure** failure of this particular intervention. Her inventory of such is included in Figure 19.1.

> ...time-out should be served up within a sterile setting – the blandest of the bland – wherein the youngster cannot see what is going on in the family...

Time-Out for Teens

As previously mentioned, some youth are too big/old for traditional time-out. But, there **is** an adaptation (Rimm, 1995). Upon commencement of arguing or primeval ranting by a teen, you can time *yourself* out – behind the locked door of your choosing (providing you have a back-up family member, such as a spouse, at home during this time – in the case of a RAD youth). Thus, you as the parent are spared from having the adolescent chase you around the house with an endless list of arguments/excuses/pleadings. Often, a maltreated young person will target one parent over the other, to more thoroughly harass. Thus, allowing the more *victimized* parent to go into time-out can be very effective.

The Navy Seal Parent

One of the special forces of our military is the Navy Seals. This elite team, usually composed of six people, are highly trained operatives who are not heavily armed. Their forte is speed and stealth. The strategy of the Navy Seals is to **get in**, accomplish the mission, and then **get out**.

Mistakes in Using Time Outs

- When children go to time-out, they often slam the **door**. We respond by telling them not to **slam** the door. Youth thus realize they have **power** over us, and continue to slam the door...

- Sometimes, when youngsters call out and ask how much time they have left, we make the mistake of talking to or actually **arguing** with them. *Conversation cancels the beneficial effects of time-out...*

- Some of us are hesitant about locking the door and will hold it closed, or not even close it at **all**. If we **hold** the door, the child **knows** we are holding the door; thus the power struggle continues. If it is not closed at all, the kiddo walks in and out, proving that we are not in control. (Note: most states' foster care regulations prohibit door-locking during time-out. For adoptive or biologic youth, let it **eat**!)

- On occasion during time-out, children throw items around their rooms. We then insist they go back to pick up what has been tossed about. Another power struggle ensues, in which case the youngsters again take charge of us – via another argument.

- Perhaps we use a time-out only after we've yelled, screamed, and lost our temper. That's too **late**. Time-out has to be executed calmly, showing that we – not the **child** – are in charge.

Adapted from: Rimm, Sylvia. *Why Bright Kids Get Poor Grades* (1995).

Figure 19.1   Mistakes in Using Time-Outs

As parents, we need a similar Navy Seal dynamic. When disciplining our kids – in situations wherein they have clearly broken a rule – we need to **get in** and **get out**. The youngster already knows the rules and consequences; there is no need to re-verbalize them. All we need to do is calmly and quietly state that the consequence is now in force. For instance, if Heather fails to bring her assignment sheet home from school, we can respond, "Oh, bummer. Looks like no privileges for the rest of the day." We don't belabor the offense or the consequence. We **get in** and **get out**.

Grounding

I use a broad definition of grounding: "the restriction of a youth's freedom, for a specific time period, or until certain conditions are satisfied" (Kaye, 1994).

Most of us were grounded from time to time while growing up. And, most of us as parents have also used this intervention with our own kiddoes also. Grounding – similar to time-out – is highly dependent upon technique. (Another caveat: with moderate to severe RAD youngsters, this particular behavioral intervention may yield lean results.) But for the rest of *youthdom*, an effective use of proper grounding technique can be extremely helpful.

Simply put, the error most of us as parents make with grounding is restricting a youngster for *too long* at a time. This form of discipline should occur, generally speaking, over 1 to 3 days at **most**. Usually, no more than a single day. Thus, when restricting a youth (for example, from outside activities) for 6 weeks at a time, we have already fumbled the ball. Such long durations merely set a kiddo up for the *Lifer Syndrome*. So however good they are immediately afterwards, it matters not. "I'm grounded for 6 weeks; so, I have no incentive to do better – I'm a *Lifer*."

Much better is to ground a youngster from _____ (fill in the blank – TV time, phone, *Nintendo*, outside free time, the car) for a day. We can then say to the youth, "Mark, I have bad news and good news. The bad news is that because of your rudeness to me just now, you are grounded from the TV and *GameCube* for the rest of the day. The good news is: tomorrow's a new **day**."

Spanking

The use of corporal punishment is frequently frowned upon by many in the mental health field. Among mainstream Americans however it is my perception that an appropriate use of spanking is well accepted. The Bible even speaks of such: "He who spares his rod hates his son, but he who loves him disciplines him diligently." Proverbs 13:24.

While I personally approve of the **judicious** usage of spanking by emotionally healthy parents, this form of discipline in the hands of an mentally unbalanced adult is scary to me. Most of us have seen, for example, parents who spank at the drop of a hat, and for every little thing. This I obviously abhor. Therefore, there are five caveats for corporal punishment that I advocate – generally without exception:

- Never spank in anger
- Never spank a child above the age of 10
- Only spank for acts of willful disobedience
- Never spank a foster child
- Spank sparingly, surrounded by several other forms of non-corporal discipline

Morning Routine

A frequent locus of tension between parents and youth is the morning routine: getting up and going each day. The key here is to put the responsibility on *Heather* to get up, get dressed, gather books and supplies, eat breakfast, and make it to the bus stop on time. Again, Dr. Sylvia Rimm (1990) has provided some advice for taking much of the mayhem out of morning battles. (Again, for moderate to severe RAD youth, this technique will likely **not** work.) Also, for any child, expect morning matters to initially get worse before they get better. The youngster is testing your resolve.

In her book, *How To Parent So Children Will Learn* (1990), Dr. Rimm has a short section entitled "Habits That Facilitate Achievement" – containing tips for taking the chaos out of the morning ritual. Obviously, as parents, we should aid Heather in learning to organize her school supplies, papers, and what-not the night before – to streamline next morning's routine.

> The key here is to put the responsibility on *Heather* to get up, get dressed, gather books and supplies, eat breakfast, and make it to the bus stop on time.

Rimm's tips for managing the morning routine are found in Figure 19.2.

Behavior Modification

In addition to medications for nocturnal bed-wetting (see Chapter 14), any of several behavior modification programs for enuresis can be highly effective, assuming that organic factors such as urinary/urethral anomalies have been ruled out by a pediatrician and/or urologist.

One effective treatment for enuresis is a simple reward system. Each morning the youngster wakes up dry, he collects points toward a

> One effective treatment for enuresis is a simple reward system.

new video game or book, for example. Some children respond better to being rewarded that **morning**; so small/simple awards are fine, as well.

Morning Routine

Step 1: Announce to your children the new guidelines for morning routines. From this day forth, *they* will be responsible for getting themselves ready for school. Your job will be to await them at the breakfast table for a pleasant morning chat, should they so choose.

Step 2: Night-before preparations include supervising the laying out of their clothes, getting books in the backpack, and setting the alarm early enough to allow plenty of morning time. They will feel just as tired at 7:00 a.m. as they will at 6:30, but the earlier start will help prevent the usual chaos. Taking youngsters to the store, allowing them to pick out their new alarm clock will serve to help usher in the new routine. Children as young as 4 years-old may use their own alarm clock.

Step 3: Kiddoes wake themselves up (absolutely no calls from others), wash, dress and pick up their room (as itemized in their guide lines checklist – see Step 1 above). Breakfast comes only when they are ready for school. Absolutely no nagging!

Step 4: A pleasant family breakfast and conversation about the day ahead! You remain at the breakfast table, leisurely sipping coffee, waiting for breakfast together – should the child so choose.

Adapted from: Rimm, Sylvia. *How to Parents So Children Will Learn* (1990).

Figure 19.2 Morning Routines

While doing my internship at the University of Nebraska Medical Center, I did a rotation at the pediatric urology clinic there in 1982. I had occasion to treat an 8 year-old boy for enuresis. We set up a very simple behavioral modification system for him. Such entailed rewarding him for staying dry. A chart was put up in the bathroom where Michael would easily see it. Every morning Michael woke up dry, he received a quarter. He also got a nickel every time he sat on the toilet. His 2-year bout with enuresis cleared up after 2 weeks.

Another alternative to combat wetting is the old bell and pad alarm which awakens the child after he wets the bed. The kiddo learns, via conditioning, over a short period of time, to awaken **himself** once his bladder fills up. He can then get up and go to the bathroom on his **own**. More information is available on the bell and pad method/device at www.bedwettingproducts.com.

Finally, verbal praise for not wetting is also frequently effective for a non-RAD youngster struggling with enuresis.

Cell Phone Therapy

This technique works within many different environments. It not only can be adapted to the **school** setting – but also to church services, club meetings, the neighbor's house, or any other situation wherein the child needs behavioral tweaking.

For this technique, the **instant** Mark acts up in class, fails to turn in an assignment, or displays inappropriate behavior, he is directed into the hallway to dial up his parent on the adult's cell phone, and explain to his mom or dad exactly what has transpired – and **why** (Blue, 2000).

The immediacy of this intervention, coupled with the mortifying effect of having the child talk

> The immediacy of this intervention, coupled with the mortifying effect of having the child talk directly to his parent...frequently renders this method effective...

directly to his parent, while at school or away from the hacienda – as well as having been singled out among his peers – frequently renders this method effective in dealing with maladaptive behaviors away from home.

Take Your Parent to School Day

It is amazing how Heather finds the internal resources to change a problem behavior once a parent chaperons her to school for the day (Dobson, 1978). To do this, we accompany our child to each of her classes, quietly sitting in the back of the room. Simply prearrange with teachers/principal ahead of time. Most will welcome your intervention.

> This is one of the most sure-fire *one-trial learning* gigs for kiddoes...I have found.

You need not say a word the entire period, or *day*. Being there – just *being there* – does the trick. This is one of the most sure-fire *one-trial learning* gigs for kiddoes (especially teens) I have found.

Martial Arts

We may also want to consider Tae Kwan Do/martial arts for a maltreated youth. Now, I know right about now you are experiencing temporal lobe seizure activity at the mere **thought** of this notion, fearing such will only make your youngster a more accomplished fighter. Well, Mark is *already* aggressive, without benefit of the Chuck Norris School of Smash.

Actually, the issue here is one of directing the kiddo's energies along socially acceptable pathways – not to mention the development of general self-discipline. And, marital arts instruction can be an ideal training ground, emphasizing: greater self-confidence, enhanced interpersonal cooperation, good sportsmanship, frustration tolerance, impulse control, gratification delay, personal discipline, sound judgment, appropriate self-sacrifice, and better goal-setting. By the way, these traits constitute a veritable *Who's Who* of healthy pre-frontal lobe function. Martial arts classes also teach the when/where/why of fighting, which can go a long way toward **reducing** your youngster's pugnacious proclivities.

911 Therapy

Escalating aggression on the part of a youth should be handled by the police. None of you should have to worry about being physically abused by another person, whether you're 8 or **88**. It also helps to have a videotape medley of the youngster's mayhem to *show* police officers, lest your darling attempt to charmingly deny his misdeeds upon their arrival, acting as if he is the second-coming of Fred Rogers. Believe me, these kiddoes can change demeanors on a dime, depending on their audience. You know what I'm talking about here. We need to make very clear to the child or teen that calling the *gendarmes* **will be** the course of action, any time he decides to become physically abusive. Then, dial 911.

> None of you should have to worry about being physically abused by another person, whether you're 8 or **88**.

Re-direction

For children or teens exhibiting pre-frontal lobe compromise (see Chapter 4), the technique of re-direction is vital. As in real estate, we have the importance of *Location/Location/Location*. Likewise, with many brain impaired young persons, we have the importance of *Re-direction/Re-direction/Re-direction*. And, such is most effectively utilized within the early/prodromal phase of a potential ballistic episode. Once a tantrum gets going, re-direction is near **worthless**.

Another important component for these youngsters is maintaining routine and structure. Anytime a pre-frontal lobe underdevelopment is present for a young person, routines are next to Godliness.

Rewards for Fun and Profit

While many interventions involve the application of **adverse** consequences in response to misbehavior, another approach in treating oppositionalism/defiance for Heather is to *catch her* performing adaptive behaviors – and reward accordingly. Such can be done via verbal praise, extended privileges, or more tangible goods such as money/a small gift. Said method also serves to teach her that life includes consequences **and** rewards.

The problem here is that too many of our youth produce a dearth of acceptable behaviors. But, once perhaps their little biochemical aquarium is cleansed out – via appropriate medications (see Chapter 14), their behavior begins to **improve**. This is typically the optimal time to pounce on praise and rewards.

Many parents perceive rewards as *bribes*. Rewards are *earned*. Bribes are **not**. How many of us, as adults, receive a paycheck at our jobs? Do we ever state, "Hey, Honey, it's payday today. I may be a little late getting home – I need to go by the bank and cash my *bribe*."? Of **course** not.

Referential Speaking

A word of praise to a spouse or other adult regarding your youngster, within the child's ear-shot, can do a world of good. This is called *Referential Speaking*, and is extremely powerful (Rimm, 1995). Such helps create motivation for what it is we are praising, and will help foster self-esteem as well.

Parent Texts

The **wise** mom/dad of a maltreated kiddo will have a *number* of resources on hand for ideas, tips, and moral support. Each of the following books is *reader friendly*, affording parents a quick and useful refresher – lest anyone should ever visit the Tolkienesque locale known as **Wit's End** (Blue, 2001).

However, as I mentioned earlier in this book, let us not make the mistake of believing that *any* single text on parenting or discipline constitutes the *end-all*. There **is** no *one* book. There **is** no *one* author. Read *several* books, picking and choosing a hodgepodge of techniques that dove-tail with your temperament, your son's or daughter's temperament, and that resonate with your own wisdom. These books should be read under a sense of prayerful discernment – allowing the Holy Spirit a chance to speak to you.

Below is a list of my personal favorites:

How to Parent So Children Will Learn. Sylvia B. Rimm, Crown Publishing, 1990.

Parenting With Love and Logic: Teaching Children Responsibility. Foster Cline, M.D., and Jim Fay, NavPress, 1990.

Personality Plus: How to Understand Others by Understanding Yourself. Florence Littauer, Fleming H. Revell Co., 1992.

Parenting Teens With Love and Logic: Preparing Adolescents for Responsible Adulthood. Foster Cline, M.D., and Jim Fay, NavPress, 1993.

Family Rules: Raising Responsible Children. Kenneth Kaye, St. Martin's Paperbacks, 1994.

Why Bright Kids Get Poor Grades: And What You Can Do About It. Sylvia B. Rimm, Crown Publishing, 1995.

When Love is Not Enough: A Guide to Parenting Children with RAD

— *Reactive Attachment Disorder*. Nancy Thomas, Families by Design, 1997.

Adopting the Hurt Child: Hope for Families with Special-Needs Kids: A Guide for Parents and Professionals. Gregory C. Keck, and Regina M. Kupecky, NavPress, 1998.

Building the Bonds of Attachment: Awaking Love in Foster and Adopted Children. Daniel Hughes, Jason Aronson Publishers, 1998.

Help for the Hopeless Child: A Guide for Families. Ronald S. Federici, Federici & Associates, 1998.

Can This Child Be Saved? Solutions For Adoptive and Foster Families. Foster Cline, M.D., and Cathy Helding, World Enterprises LLC, 1999.

Parenting the Hurt Child: Helping Adoptive Families Heal and Grow. Gregory C. Keck, and Regina M. Kupecky, Pinon Press, 2002.

Summary

Parents should approach child-raising with a ready arsenal of behavioral techniques. The task of adolescence, for example, is to push parental boundaries as far as possible. Remember your **own** teen years? Rather than frontally engaging each battle, pick and choose the most important issues to consequence. We then can pull out a particular intervention – appropriate for the occasion – and **calmly** reinforce limits via our actions, rather than our words.

The Maltreated Child

Part IV

Nautical Coordinates

Chapter 20

Underwater Sleuthing: A Sample Report

So as to give you a sampling of what to expect from a thorough neuropsychologic examination, I submit the following report of a recent young adolescent male patient of mine. Obviously, his name and that of past and present treating professionals have been changed to protect confidentiality.

Neuropsychologic Evaluation

NAME: John Doe
AGE: 13 years – 10 months   **DOB:** 8/2/88   **GRADE:** 9th
DATES OF EVALUATION: 6/12/02

Reason for Referral

John is described as selfish, obnoxious, rude, manipulative, and controlling. He also exhibits bossiness, oppositionalism, verbal/physical aggression, lying, externalization of blame, and academic amotivation – inclusive of failure to complete assignments. In addition, the young man presents with a history of sexual inappropriateness and regressive behavior (e.g., wanting to be rocked/fed/bathed by his adoptive mother). Although the patient does not currently receive counseling, he participates in a weekend camp with Jane Counselor, MS, LPC, x every other month. He previously worked with Joan Psychologist, Ph.D., x approximately 1 year. A neuropsychologic re-evaluation is requested in order to update the differential diagnoses and to assist in further treatment planning.

Procedures

Lateral Dominance Examination	Gordon Diagnostic System
Bender Visual-Motor Gestalt Test	Attention Deficit Hyperactivity Weighting Scale
Trail Making Test	Selective Verbal Learning Test
Wechsler Intelligence Scale for Children—III	Abstract Visual Memory Test
Woodcock-Johnson Tests of Achievement—Revised	Littauer Personality Profile
Gray Writing Samples Test	Personality Inventory of Children
Stroop Color-Word Test	Randolph Attachment Disorder Questionnaire
Coding—Incidental Learning Test	Thematic Apperception Test—Gray Adaptation
Reitan-Klove Tactile Finger Recognition Test	Rorschach Inkblot Technique
Reitan-Klove Fingertip Number Writing Test	Review of Records
Speech Sounds Perception Test	Adoptive Parent Interview
Seashore Rhythm Test	Adolescent Interview
Test of Auditory Discrimination	Behavioral Observations

Pertinent History

John is the product of a chaotic FOO, initially removed from the birth home at 6 months of age due to neglect, as well as physical/sexual abuse. At that point, the patient entered several foster care placements x 5½ years, prior to coming to live with Don and Jenny Doe in 12/94. Adoption consummation occurred 4/95 at age 6½. In 11/96, the Does divorced. Subsequently, John's adoptive mother re-married, to Mr. Jerry White.

The current home consists of John; Mr. and Ms. White, along with their 2 biologic offspring: Peter – 5 and Paul – 2. The patient's half-sister, Mary – 15, has been living with the adoptive father since

12/01, while two other half-siblings: Tina – 18 and Marilyn – 16, reside in a foster domicile.

Regarding birth history, parental ETOH/drug abuse is reported, calling for the need to R/O in utero alcohol/drug exposure. Developmental milestones are said to have been delayed: crawling – 12 months; walking – 2 years; simple sentences – 3 years; and toilet training – 4 years.

Medical history is remarkable for: admission to Midwest Hospital in Southwest City at 6 months of age, secondary to physical abuse (multiple fractures to the lower extremities, as well as a reported mild Closed Head Injury); chicken pox at age 5; fractured left wrist in 11/98 (reportedly resulting from a fall while playing); laceration to the right hand requiring sutures at age 13, and environmental allergies.

Mental health history includes: Depressive Disorder NOS of Childhood with Borderline Psychosis; RAD; ODD; ADHD; and Learning Disorder NOS. Family mental health history is reportedly remarkable for "mental problems," as well as the previously mentioned ETOH/drug abuse. In addition, diagnoses for the patient's half-sibling – Mary, includes: ODD; Anxiety Disorder NOS of Childhood; RAD; and Learning Disorder NOS.

John has been promoted to 9th grade at Suburban High School. He was retained in Kindergarten due to immaturity. The young man was returned to public education in 2/01 after 3 years of home schooling. During the 2001/2002 academic year, he carried a Special Ed coding of ED. The patient was mainstreamed in all subjects, reportedly receiving prn Content Mastery, with modified curricula in Language Arts. Final marks for Spring 2002 included: Art – 78; Science – 76; History – 75; Language Arts – 73; Business Support Systems – 70; Language Exploration – 70; and Math – 70.

During the 2001/2002 academic term, the adolescent exhibited academic amotivation – inclusive of failure to complete assignments. According to Ms. White, John's grades were "terrible" – reportedly having declined since 12/01. In addition, he displayed disrespect toward authority figures, as well as verbal/physical aggression – receiving several ISSs/OSSs for fighting, assaulting a teacher, and writing a "nasty letter."

As to peer/sibling relations, the teen is described as selfish, obnoxious, rude, argumentative, manipulative, and controlling. He also exhibits bossiness, oppositionalism, verbal/physical aggression, lying, as well as externalization of blame. In addition, the young man is said to act in an immature fashion via showing off/clowning around. According to Adoptive Mom, "John will have friends for a little while – until they tire of his antics and shun him."

Furthermore, there is said to be a highly conflictual relationship between John and half-sister, Mary. The situation has been additionally strained by the fact that Mary reportedly went through a "manic" phase in 5/01 – requiring several hospitalizations and an eventual RTC placement – which was "very hard on John." Moreover, Adoptive Father took custody of Mary in 12/01, which is said to have left the patient "very angry."

In addition, numerous incidents of sexual misconduct have been reported for John, including the inappropriate touching of male peers in Kindergarten and 3rd grade, along with an 8/00 sexual molestation of the White's oldest son (age 3 at the time); however, no charges were filed. Such conduct has continued this past year wherein John is said to have inappropriately touched an MR child, as well as an 18 year-old female. According to Ms. White, "He masturbates a lot, and touches others. He doesn't think before hitting someone or sexually touching them…"

The patient is also perceived as unbonded with his adoptive mother and step-father. Ms. White states, "John is frequently argumentative, manipulative, and controlling. He doesn't seem to belong to us. I want to make him feel that he is a part of us, but he doesn't fit in. I feel he is just waiting to be removed." In addition, "John's affection does not seem genuine. He only hugs me when he wants something. Also, when I try to give him the kind of attention a loving mother would give her son, he resorts to being a baby…"

Moreover, Ms. White states, "I'm afraid of John. He seems to be struggling with his identity, and appears so confused that I'm fearful he is going to *snap*. We cannot seem to get to the core of his problems. I am worried we are not helping John get better."

Adoptive Mom also reports a recent "return to the picture" for Adoptive Father, Mr. Don Doe, after an approximate 3-year absence. According to Ms. White, "John is more aggressive and depressed – crying often and sleeping a lot, following visits with his adoptive father. He is also going through a *woe is me* stage, trying to adapt to Mr. Doe taking Mary and not him."

Discipline methods at home include: time-outs, loss of privileges, removal of toys, and extra chores – all ineffective. According to Ms. White, "John is impervious to punishment and could care less about any type of discipline."

The patient has his own bedroom, wherein no sleep disturbances are noted. As to appetite, the teen eats very little nutritiously sound victuals, preferring junk food.

Favored activities include: drawing, reading horror stories, as well as "sleeping." The patient also attends worship services/Sunday School/youth group with his adoptive family, wherein he is described as easily bored and inattentive. Furthermore, complaints of rudeness and disrespect toward others there are noted.

Current Medications

Medication	Reason Prescribed	Dosage	Date Began	Efficacy	Prescribing Physician
Risperdal	Aggression	.25 mg bid	6/02	Moderate	Richard Psychiatrist, M.D.

Previous Medications

Medication	Reason Prescribed	Dosage	Date Began	Date DCed	Reason for DC	Prescribing Physician
Ritalin	ADHD	10 mg bid	1993	Unkn	Ineffective	Richard Psychiatrist, MD
Dexedrine SR	ADHD	Unkn	Unkn	Unkn	Refused to Take	Richard Psychiatrist, MD
Clonidine	Aggression	.025 mg qd	1996	4/02	Severe Night Terrors	Richard Psychiatrist, MD
Wellbutrin SR	Depression	150 mg qd	Unkn	Unkn	"Seemed Better"	Richard Psychiatrist, MD
Adderall	ADHD	20 mg bid	Unkn	Unkn	Ineffective	Richard Psychiatrist, MD
Seroquel	Rages	25 mg prn	Unkn	Unkn	"No Longer Needed"	Richard Psychiatrist, MD
Effexor XR	Unknown	37.5 mg qd	Unkn	Unkn	Unknown	Richard Psychiatrist, MD
Zyprexa	Sleep	2.5 mg q hs	3/99	3/01	"No Longer Needed"	Richard Psychiatrist, MD
Celexa	Depression	20 mg qd	2/02	Unkn	"Too Outgoing"	Richard Psychiatrist, MD

Behavioral Observations

John is a 13 year – 10 month-old Hispanic/American male of average height/slender build, with thick/curly black hair, brown eyes, and pleasant facial features. He is dressed in white T-shirt with cowboy logo screened across the front, tan shorts, white socks, and brown shoes. The young man also sports a black tether band on the left wrist. He exhibits coryza symptoms, including upper respiratory sniffles.

Testing begins at 9:10 a.m. with several brief procedures prior to the WISC-III. Motoric activity reveals minor sporadic fidgeting. Attention/concentration are age appropriate, at least on a one-to-one basis. Mood impresses as overtly euthymic, with something of a curious affect – i.e., a fixed smile emblazoned upon John's facies throughout. Attitude is compliant but quiet throughout the day. Upon completion of the WISC-III, six tests assessing ADHD are completed, at which time lethargy is observed.

Subsequent to a 35-minute lunch break, the WJ-R is conducted, followed by GWST, TAT-GA, and then the Rorschach.

Clinical Interview

Mood continues to impress as overtly euthymic, with the above-stated curious affect. Eye contact is WNL. Speech is quiet, but otherwise age-appropriate. I estimate verbal intellect as within the upper bounds of the Average range (i.e., approximately an 105), via my interaction with him.

John was recently promoted to 9th grade. He states Art is a favored subject, while Math is said to be least preferred – with failing grades during the first two semesters. He admits receiving an ISS x 3 days for hitting another student, as well as two OSSs for assaulting a teacher "by mistake" – once following an altercation with a peer, and again for "writing a nasty letter."

The teen names "Jonathan" and "Jared" as best friends, while noting "Anna" to be an acquaintance with whom he plays chess and ping-pong at a local recreational center.

Extracurricular activities include computer games, drawing, Legos, and videos. The young man states he recently signed up to participate in soccer during the upcoming academic year. He also mentions plans to visit family members in San Antonio within the next few weeks.

As to home-life, the patient acknowledges disciplinary action "every day," typically for lying, failure to complete chores, or attempting to avoid responsibility for his actions. John also notes that his Legos "were taken up," but claims he cannot recall the specific circumstances.

Additionally, the young man discloses strained relations with 15 year-old half-sister, Mary, stating, " I think she's psycho. She acts *crazy*." Relations with his adoptive parents are reportedly good, despite reports of regular verbal castigation by them, secondary to his own misdeeds.

John's evaluation concludes at 4:00 p.m.

Previous Test Results

A neuropsychologic assessment performed by our clinic on 2/99 (CA of 10 years – 6 months and 4th grade) revealed the following WISC-III data: VIQ – 81; PIQ – 108; FIQ – 93 (Average range). However, an estimated constitutional VIQ of 97 (Average range) was produced.

A second neuropsychologic assessment performed by our clinic, on 9/00 (CA of 11 years – 3 months and 5th grade) yielded the following WISC-III SSs: VIQ – 78; PIQ – 94; FIQ – 84 (Low Average range). Again, an estimated constitutional VIQ of 97 (Average range) emerged.

Current Test Results

Lateral Dominance

	Motor Praxis Items	Extremities	Preference
2/99	10 out of 10	Right Upper/Lower	Right
9/00	10 out of 10	Right Upper/Lower	Right
6/02	10 out of 10	Right Upper/Lower	Right

Bender-Gestalt

	Errors	Visual-Motor Integration Age	Chronologic Age	Delay	Markers
2/99	1	Age-Appropriate	10 years—6 months	None	Circles for dots (1) – Histrionics/Immaturity
9/00	0	Age-Appropriate	12 years—7 months	None	WNL
6/02	0	Age-Appropriate	13 years—10 months	None	WNL

Trail Making

	Part A					Part B		
	Sec-onds	Errors	Range	Markers	Sec-onds	Errors	Range	Markers
2/99	19	1	> 17 seconds = impaired	R/O Anxiety and/or Visual Spatial Deficits	45	1	> 36 seconds = impaired	Cognitive Inflexibility
9/00	49	2	> 17 seconds = impaired	R/O Anxiety and/or Visual Spatial Deficits	52	0	> 36 seconds = impaired	Cognitive Inflexibility
6/02	20	0	> 17 seconds = impaired	R/O Anxiety and/or Visual Spatial Deficits	37	3	> 36 seconds = impaired	Mild Cognitive Inflexibility

WISC-III

	2/99				9/00				6/02		
	IQ	Range	%ile		IQ	Range	%ile		IQ	Range	%ile
Verbal Scale	81	Low Average	10	Verbal Scale	78	Borderline	7	Verbal Scale	87	Low Average	19
Perform Scale	108	Average	70	Perform Scale	94	Average	34	Perform Scale	117	Above Average	87
Full Scale	93	Average	32	Full Scale	84	Low Average	14	Full Scale	101	Average	53

Verbal	2/99		9/00		6/02	
	SS	IQ Equivalent	SS	IQ Equivalent	SS	IQ Equivalent
Information	4	65	7	85	5	70
Similarities	6	75	9	95	9	95
Arithmetic	9	95	6	75	13	118
Vocabulary	8	90	5	70	8	90
Comprehension	6	75	3	60	3	60
Digit Span	8	90	8	90	7	85

204

Performance	2/99		9/00		6/02	
	SS	IQ Equivalent	SS	IQ Equivalent	SS	IQ Equivalent
Picture Completion	10	100	7	85	13	118
Coding/Digit Symbol	7	85	3	60	9	95
Picture Arrangement	6	75	8	90	13	118
Block Design	19	170	13	118	14	125
Object Assembly	14	125	14	125	14	125

Woodcock-Johnson Revised

	Grade Equivalent			Standard Score			Percentile		
	2/99	9/00	6/02	2/99	9/00	6/02	2/99	9/00	6/02
Basic Reading	2.4	3.6	5.2	82	84	90	12	15	26
Broad Reading	3.0	6.0	6.6	84	92	93	15	30	31
Broad Mathematics	5.0	5.8	8.5	97	91	100	42	26	50
Basic Writing	3.3	4.0	6.7	85	82	90	15	11	25
Word Identification (reading recognition)	2.8	4.4	6.2	82	87	91	12	20	28
Word Attack (phonics)	2.1	2.8	4.1	82	83	89	11	13	23
Passage Comprehension (reading comprehension)	3.3	7.6	6.9	90	101	95	25	54	38
Calculation (computational math)	4.5	5.4	8.3	104	87	99	29	19	48
Applied Problems (story problems)	5.4	6.3	8.7	109	96	100	57	41	50
Punctuation/Capitalization Knowledge	3.3	3.3	6.3	88	78	93	22	8	33
Spelling/Sight-Word Vocabulary	2.7	4.3	5.8	80	84	90	9	15	25
Verb/Noun Usage	2.9	4.0	5.4	86	85	89	17	16	24

Stroop

	Word	Color	Color-Word	Range	Markers
2/99	42	42	43	Mean = 50, SD = 10	WNL
9/00	38	39	33	Mean = 50, SD = 10	R/O Dyslexia/Bradyphrenia/Visual Inattention
6/02	39	41	50	Mean = 50, SD = 10	Mild Visual Inattention

Gray Writing Samples

	2/99 Errors	2/99 Markers	9/00 Errors	9/00 Markers	6/02 Errors	6/02 Markers
Spelling	10	Low Average Range Graphics	1	Low Average Range Graphics	3	Borderline Graphic Dyspraxia
Letter Reversals	1	Mild L/R Droop	1	Mild L/R Droop	0	No L/R Droop
Capitalization	5	WNL Content	1	WNL Content	0	WNL Content
Spacing	1	Spelling Dyspraxia	5	Dyslexia	2	Mild Dyslexia
Punctuation	1	R/O Borderline Dyslexia	3	Mid 4th Grade Quality	1	Early 6th Grade Quality
Sentence Run-ons	0	Early 3rd Grade Quality	0		0	
Sentence Fragments	2		0		0	
Verb/Noun Usage	0		2		1	
Carelessness	1		8		42	

Coding – Incidental Learning

Paired Associate Symbol Recall

	Raw Score	Range	Markers
2/99	N/A	N/A	N/A
9/00	N/A	N/A	N/A
6/02	15 out of 18	Mean = 11, SD = 5	WNL

Free Recall

	Raw Score	Range	Markers
2/99	N/A	N/A	N/A
9/00	N/A	N/A	N/A
6/02	9 out of 9	Mean = 8, SD = 2	WNL

Paired Associate Digit Recall

	Raw Score	Range	Markers
2/99	N/A	N/A	N/A
9/00	N/A	N/A	N/A
6/02	6 out of 18	Mean = 12, SD = 5	Verbal Memory Deficit/Left Tertiary Integration Region

Tactile Finger Recognition

	Right Hand	Left Hand	Range	Markers
2/99	0	4	$\geq$ 4 total = Impaired	Mild Tactile Inattention
9/00	2	0	$\geq$ 4 total = Impaired	WNL
6/02	0	0	$\geq$ 4 total = Impaired	WNL

Fingertip Number Writing

	Right Hand	Left Hand	Range	Markers
2/99	7	9	$\geq$ 4 total = Impaired	Tactile Inattention
9/00	6	9	$\geq$ 4 total = Impaired	Tactile Inattention
6/02	2	2	$\geq$ 4 total = Impaired	Mild Tactile Inattention

Speech Sounds

	Errors	Range	Markers
2/99	10	> 10 errors = Impaired	WNL
9/00	8	> 10 errors = Impaired	WNL
6/02	9	> 10 errors = Impaired	WNL

Seashore Rhythm

	Correct	Range	Markers
2/99	19	< 24 correct = Impaired	Auditory Inattention
9/00	22	< 24 correct = Impaired	Auditory Inattention
6/02	23	< 24 correct = Impaired	Auditory Inattention

TAD

Quiet Subtest

	Errors	Percentile	Standard Score	Range	Markers
2/99	2	26th	90	Average	Auditory/Visual Distractibility
9/00	2	22nd	89	Low Average	Auditory/Visual Distractibility
6/02	0	100th	<139	Very Superior	WNL

Noise Subtest

	Errors	Percentile	Standard Score	Range	Markers
2/99	11	19th	87	Low Average	Auditory/Visual Distractibility
9/00	8	48th	99	Average	Mild Auditory/ Visual Distractibility
6/02	9	31st	92	Average	Auditory/Visual Distractibility

Gordon

Delay Subtest

	Efficiency Ratio	Total Correct
2/99	.88 (WNL)	43 (Borderline)
9/00	.51 (Abnormal)	37 (Abnormal)
6/02	.79 (Borderline)	57 (WNL)

Vigilance Subtest

	Total Commissions	Total Correct
2/99	18 (Abnormal)	41 (Borderline)
9/00	2 (WNL)	11 (Abnormal)
6/02	1 (WNL)	44 (WNL)

Distractibility Subtest

	Total Commissions	Total Correct
2/99	82 (Abnormal)	16 (Abnormal)
9/00	78 (Abnormal)	18 (Abnormal)
6/02	1 (WNL)	40 (WNL)

Attention Deficit Hyperactivity Weighting Scale

Modality	Weighting	Modality	Weighting
TESTING SESSION		**GORDON**	
Fidgets/Impulsive		Delay	
Motoric Over-Activity		Vigilance	
Poor Attention		Distractibility	
SCHOOL SETTING		Commission Errors	
Fidgets/Impulsive		**TAD**	
Motoric Over-Activity		Quiet	
Poor Attention	2	Distractibility	2
PIC		**STROOP**	
ADHD		Word	1
LITTAUER		Color	
Primary Sanguine	3	Color-Word	
Secondary Sanguine		**SPEECH SOUNDS**	
WISC-III		Distractibility	
Arithmetic		**SEASHORE RHYTHM**	
Digit Span	1	Distractibility	2
Coding	1	**REITAN-KLOVE TACTILE**	
Picture Completion		Distractibility	
		Distractibility	1
		TOTAL	13

2/99	9/00	6/02
23/Severe Range	**21/Severe Range**	**13/Mild Range**

0	—	12	=	WNL
13	—	**16**	=	**Mild Range**
17	—	20	=	Moderate Range
21	—	↑	=	Severe Range

209

Selective Verbal Learning

	Standard Score	Percentile	IQ Equivalent	Range	Markers
2/99	N/A	N/A	N/A	N/A	N/A
9/00	N/A	N/A	N/A	N/A	N/A
6/02	6	50th	75	Borderline	Verbal Memory/Left Temporo-Parietal Tertiary

Abstract Visual Memory

	Standard Score	Percentile	IQ Equivalent	Range	Markers
2/99	N/A	N/A	N/A	N/A	N/A
9/00	N/A	N/A	N/A	N/A	N/A
6/02	10	50th	100	Average	WNL

Littauer

	Primary	Secondary
2/99	Sanguine	Phlegmatic
9/00	Sanguine	Phlegmatic
6/02	Sanguine	Co-Choleric/Melancholy

RADQ

	Raw Score	Range	Markers
2/99	N/A	N/A	N/A
9/00	88	> 65 = Abnormal	RAD
6/02	107	> 65 = Abnormal	RAD

Cerebral Cortex Localization

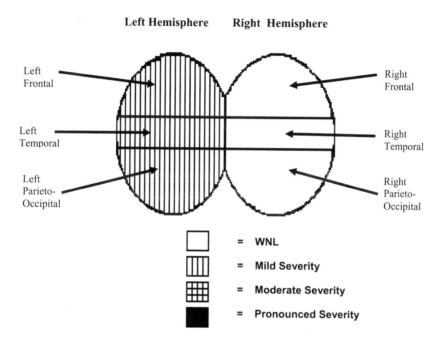

Left Hemisphere   Right Hemisphere

Left Frontal — Right Frontal

Left Temporal — Right Temporal

Left Parieto-Occipital — Right Parieto-Occipital

□ = WNL

▥ = Mild Severity

▦ = Moderate Severity

■ = Pronounced Severity

211

PIC

T-Scores	20	30	40	50	60	70	80	90	100	110	120

	Normal Range	Abnormal Range

Code	Label	T-Score
L		30
F	"Parental Drain"	106
DEF	Indices	56
ADJ		105
ACH		69
IS	Learning Triad	31
DVL		55
SOM	Histrionics	44
D	Childhood Depression	100
FAM	FOO Conflict	53
DLQ	Narcissism	99
WDL	Atypical Depression	95
ANX	Anxiety/Insecurity	69
PSY	Borderline Conditions	117
HPR	ADHD	76
SSK	Social Skills	89

T-Scores	20	30	40	50	60	70	80	90	100	110	120

TAT-GA

2/99	9/00	6/02			6/02
80%	100%	90%	Punitive Consequences *Hit Rate*		
		< 90%	Punitive Consequences *Hit Rate* = abnormal range		
0	0		R/O STD	x	1
0	0		R/O Histrionics	x	1
0	0		R/O Depression	x	1
0	0		R/O Psychosexual Maladjustment	x	0
0	0		R/O Denial	x	1

Rorschach

	2/99	9/00	6/02		
X-	= .38	= .29	.35 **	(>.33 = abnormal range)	Mild Perceptual Distortion
X+	= .38 **	= .38 **	.26 **	(<.45 = abnormal range)	Mild Perceptual Distortion
Populars	= 4	= 7	2 **	(< 5 = abnormal range)	Mild Perceptual Distortion
M-	= 1	= 0	1 **	(≥ 1 = abnormal range)	Mild Perceptual Distortion
SS	= 11	= 12 **	7	(≥ 8 = abnormal range)	Subtle Thought Disorder
Fr	= 2**	= 2 **	3 **	(≥ 1 = abnormal range)	Narcissism
AG	= 1	= 0	1	(≥ 2 = abnormal range)	Unresolved Anger
Mor	= 2	= 3 **	3 **	(≥ 2 = abnormal range)	Depression
C´	= 2	= 1	2 **	(≥ 2 = abnormal range)	Depression
V	= 0	= 0	0	(≥ 1 = abnormal range)	Depression
m	= 2	= 0	1	(≥ 2 = abnormal range)	Anxiety
Y	= 0	= 1	1	(≥ 2 = abnormal range)	Anxiety
Sx	= 0	= 0	0	(≥ 2 = abnormal range)	Psychosexual Maladjustment

** Clinically Significant Range

Super-Ego/*Conscience* Index

76%	Super-Ego/*Conscience* Index
< **90**%	Super-Ego/*Conscience* Index = abnormal range
40% - 75%	Super-Ego Structure (*Conscience*) Underdevelopment
	• Frequently correlates with Narcissism
	• 95% probability of full development within 2 – 4 years
0% - 39%	"Absent" Super-Ego Structure (*Conscience*)
	• Frequently correlates with Sociopathy
	(a total absence of *conscience*)

213

Bipolar Conditions

Criteria	Weighting
1. Borderline Syndrome of Childhood (BSC)	
2. Borderline Psychosis of Childhood (BPC)	✓
3. Sufficient Neuropsychologic Markers	✓
4. Documentable Emotionality via Psychometric Data	✓
5. Rapid Daily Cycling/Mood Swings	
6. Chronic Irritability	✓
7. Parental History of Bipolar Disorder	✓

6/02   5/Strong Bipolar Likelihood

0	—	3	=	WNL
4	—	↑	=	Strong Bipolar Likelihood

Diagnostic Impressions

AXIS I: 313.89 Reactive Attachment Disorder with Borderline Psychotic Features

296.80 Bipolar Disorder NOS of Adolescence

313.81 Oppositional Defiant Disorder

314.01 Attention Deficit Hyperactivity Disorder

315.20 Disorder of Written Expression, inclusive of mild Dyslexia

315.00 Reading Disorder, mild

995.50 Neglect of Child, by history

995.50 Physical Abuse of Child, by history

995.50 Sexual Abuse of Child, by history

V61.20 Sexual Abuse of Child (perpetrator), by history

AXIS II: Narcissistic and Histrionic Traits

AXIS III: R/O In Utero Alcohol/Drug Exposure, by history

Mild CHI, by history

Seasonal Allergies, by history

AXIS IV: Psychosocial Stressors: Chaotic FOO replete with neglect along with physical and sexual abuse; multiple placements; loss of family members; re-emergence of adoptive father; ongoing academic problems

214

AXIS V: Current GAF: 35

Recommendations

(1)   The first order of business is to check with Dr. Psychiatrist concerning the possibility of a slight upward titration of John's Risperdal, given the continuing markers of Borderline Psychosis (BP) – virtually unchanged in severity from 2/99 and 9/00 – even on .25 mg qhs of Risperdal.

Until this syndrome is driven into remission, we might as well join Andy, Barney, and Aunt Bea out on the front porch for home-made ice cream – in terms of helping John. Furthermore, an increase in the current Risperdal regimen can also serve to address the teen's insomnia. However, I respectfully bow to Dr. Psychiatrist here.

(2)   Second, if we are truly serious about getting this young man turned around – and I think we *are* – a full-bore frontal assault on his RAD ("could care less that he has a mother," "doesn't seem to belong to us," and "can't seem to get to the core of his problems") is desperately needed. Fortunately, a world-class Bonding/Attachment psychotherapist – Ms. Jane Counselor – has already been working with the patient. So, **this** is a plus.

Unless John receives a minimum 3 week/daily regimen of Bonding/Attachment Therapy – once the BP is cleansed out of the lagoon – his prognosis is at best very guarded. Getting the BP nuked is a necessary first step in successfully implementing Bonding/Attachment Therapy! To make matters worse, Ms. White is understandably *fearful* of her son. Moreover, an intensive regimen of Bonding/Attachment Therapy can get the young man on the road toward his own identity definition – another issue on the plate ("confused as to who he is…"). Such a regimen will also serve as a springboard in addressing John's sexual acting out.

(3)   Once the Borderline Psychosis is addressed and an intensive Bonding/Attachment Therapy regimen is concluded, I would then take stock of where we are, in terms of said Bipolar Disorder of Adolescence. Then, if needed, such can be treated via any number of mood/impulse stabilizing agents, such as Depakote, Neurontin, Tegretol, or Lithium Carbonate at that time.

(4)   Another option for the young man is EEG Neurofeedback. Every year more data emerge demonstrating the efficacy of *brain re-training*, if you will, whereby actual neurologic electrical function is optimized, often with excellent results in terms of RAD, mood disturbance, and brain dysfunction. Such would not, however, displace John's need for psychopharmacology – at least initially.

(5)   As for behavioral interventions, the Whites report that time-out, loss of privileges, removal of toys, and extra chores as ineffective. With kiddoes such as John, the foundational bedrock of *any* disciplinary approach is going to be the systematic nuking of *TVG* (*Toxic Verbal Gameyness*). Although I cannot speak for Mr. and Ms. White, *most* parents in our culture choose to lecture…explain… pontificate…re-explain…debate…and *spell out* house rules over and over and over to our youth – as if they have experienced a stroke – replete with memory loss – since the **last** time we enumerated house rules for them, 10 minutes earlier! This sort of thing only serves to elevate a young person's inappropriate power-base within the home. As is known, John frequently argues with his parents. We should declare a moratorium on arguing with this boy.

Explain rules once – maybe twice. Then do not get sucked into more of this. Be *Navy Seal* parents during periods of discipline. Get in and get *out*.

(6) The Whites should also give thought to utilization of *Audio Therapy*. Such entails using a small/inexpensive micro-cassette recorder to capture episodes of verbal sassing/screaming on the part of John. Then, such can be immediately, or later on, played back for him to hear. It is very important though that such be done in a *subtly jocular/low-key* fashion by parents.

(7) Furthermore, we should consider *Videocam Therapy*. The way this works is that it is calmly explained to John that the household has been asked to provide celluloid vignettes for possible usage in the upcoming horror/comedy, *Godzilla Meets Jerry Jones* – starring Terry Bradshaw, Jim Carrey, and Whoopie Goldberg – with a brief cameo appearance by Bill Clinton.

We then keep our little camcorder within easy reach at home. On occasions wherein the youth begins to argue, spit, curse, or fume, we merely roll camera. Later on, at a time convenient for parents, a sneak-preview of the film is served up for any interested family members to watch. Provide sodas, popcorn, and dill pickles for all. Moreover, it is not necessary that John be present. However, curiosity usually gets the best of young persons here! Oh, and don't forget to keep parental tongues planted firmly in cheek with *this* one also.

(8) I would also suggest that Mr. and Ms. White take a look at the PlugHugger device, so as to grease the wheel by way of restricting John's access to electronic devices of pleasure, such as TV, radio, etc, during periods of restricted privileges. This can be obtained from Educational Assessments Services, Inc (1-800-475-1118). Another source is Home Depot at 1-800-430-3376. In addition, I have a flyer regarding this which we will give to the boy's parents.

(9) Another behavioral strategy Mr. and Ms. White should consider is *Bland Sandwich Therapy*, whereby John would be required – on days of restricted privileges – to eat a sandwich brought from home (e.g., a plain-Jane concoction consisting of, say, a slice of tomato, clump of lettuce, and dab of mustard – or peanut butter and jelly, etc), as opposed to being allowed to choose an item from the menu, should the family be dining out/doing carry-out at a pizza place, fast food joint, etc.

(10) Within the school milieu, John carried a Special Ed coding of ED during 2001/2002. He also received Content Mastery and Modified Curricula. I see both as appropriate. However, a change *is* needed in the teen's Content Mastery – from prn to 30 minutes **daily** – targeting: phonics, spelling/sight-word vocabulary, punctuation/capitalization knowledge, and basic compositional writing. Our realistic window of opportunity will be running out within the next 3 years or so, at habilitating John's neurologic LD. Thus, an all-out frontal assault in this regard is needed.

(11) Furthermore, John needs professional tutorial aid over the rest of the summer, into the Fall semester – focusing on phonics, spelling/sight-word vocabulary, punctuation/capitalization knowledge, and basic compositional writing. The summer regimen should be twice weekly 45-minute sessions, going to **one** weekly session upon start-up of 9th grade.

I cannot *overemphasize* here the need to jump on the academic habilitation **now**, while John's developmental window of access for this intervention is still available. In addition, I would point out that tutoring is typically most effective when not performed by a parent. And, our clinic can provide information to the Whites regarding the various tutoring options out there.

(12) Moreover, given that the lad exhibits academic amotivation, with declining grades since 12/01, I again – as was the case 1½ years ago – recommend we set John up on a *Motivation Plan*. Such is a structured format coordinated by parents, to inject a daily dosage of academic *want to* in a young person, in order to ameliorate MIA homework, as well as academic underproduction.

A *Motivation Plan* employs the intelligent usage of an airtight assignment sheet system, utilizing parents as gatekeepers of favorite activities. It is my experience that once we begin to incorporate some of the principles in Dr. Rimm's book, *Why Bright Kids Get Poor Grades*, within the context of a *Motivation Plan* as herein described, an elevation in *self-esteem* frequently occurs on the part of the young person, along with improved grades. And, our clinic can set this up for the Whites, within a single 2-hour session.

(13) It is also my hope that a marked improvement in the young man's anger/maladaptive behavior via the above recommendations will occur. However, should such continue (i.e., the bossiness, oppositionalism, verbal/physical aggression, lying, externalization of blame, sexually inappropriate behavior, etc), he *may* require an RTC environment x 6 months or more, in order to have a *running shot* at life. Nevertheless, I am optimistic that with proper neurochemical addressment, such a measure *can* be avoided.

As we know, the Whites have gone the 2nd, 3rd, and 4th miles with this young man. Sometimes it is simply untenable for a youth to remain within a home setting until after a 9 to 12 month stay in a high quality RTC. However, once Dr. Psychiatrist has the opportunity to create an optimal neurochemical aquarium for the young man, I think RTC intervention can be avoided.

(14) Finally, John should be re-evaluated by way of a neuropsychologic examination in 12 months, in order to continue monitoring his progress across the board vis-à-vis: overall brain development; cognitive/IQ factors; academic skill progression; the BPA; his BDA; ADHD status; the RAD; along with ongoing psychotropic management. The current and previous neuropsychologic evaluations will serve as excellent baselines for subsequent comparison.

Thank you very much for allowing me to evaluate John once again. I hope the information is helpful to him, the Whites, Suburban High School, along with Ms. Counselor, and Dr. Psychiatrist.

Steven G. Gray, Ph.D.

Steven G. Gray, Ph.D.
Diplomate, American Board of Pediatric Neuropsychology
Diplomate, American Board of Vocational Neuropsychology
Clinical Assistant Professor, University of Texas Southwestern
    Medical Center

Chapter 21

Scoping the Ocean Floor:
Test Prowlings

> **Warning**: May induce drowsiness.
> Do not drive or operate heavy
> machinery while reading.

This chapter is primarily geared toward the professional – someone who wishes a more detailed *blow-by-blow* of the technical aspects of the neuropsychologic test battery I **personally** use. Thus, parents, you have my full permission to skip this chapter, should such fall under the rubric of TMI (Too Much Information). However, feel free to read this chapter should you be a chronic insomniac.

Prelude

To identify wreckage on the bottom of the drink, I use a neuro-psychologic battery of up to 26 procedures, each measuring different brain regions/functioning. Via analyzing the results of these psychometrics and the composite picture they create, I can get an excellent idea of the underwater root causes entangling a youngster. And remember, the following are tests which have proven valuable to *me* over the last 22 years. Other pediatric neuropsychologists' batteries will differ somewhat.

Lateral Dominance Examination

This test (Reitan, 1994) reveals which side of a child's brain is *motor* dominant, and *language* dominant. Such can generally be assessed visually via fine-motor and gross-motor preferences. In this simple test, the young person writes his name, throws a ball, turns a doorknob, pretends to step on a bug, etc – to demonstrate motor dominance.

In Chapter 4, I stated that the right side of the brain controls the left side of the body – motorically, while the left side of the brain controls the right side of the body – motorically. Therefore, typically a right-handed person is left brain dominant for language. Moreover, the vast majority of left-handed persons are also left-brained for language. Roughly, only 10% of left-handed individuals are *not* left-brain dominant for language.

However, mixed dominance occurs when a youth performs *some* motor functions with the left hand, and others via the right (e.g., writing with the left hand, but throwing or kicking right).

I have used Lateral Dominance as my *lead-off batter* with kids for at least 15 years. The reasons? First, it's a very non-threatening test – a great ice-breaker with a child. Second, it's relatively fun. The youth gets to leave his seat and allows him to do *pretend* situations: throwing a baseball, kicking a football, etc. So, this test is very innocuous, and allows us to build added rapport with Mark, a process begun once we first sit down with him in the morning to chat, helping him get comfortable in the testing situation.

Bender Visual-Motor Gestalt Test

This test (Bender, 1938) measures visual-motor integration. It involves the kiddo simply copying on paper nine geometric figures (various angles and squiggles) as best she can. We simply say to the child, "I'd like you to copy each of these pictures onto your piece of paper." From her drawings – compared against standardized scoring rules tailored for specific ages – I can determine whether the lass tests out above age level, on age level, or below the anticipated ability for her age with regard to visual-motor/spatial skills.

Bender-Gestalt Cerebral Cortical Location Markers

Error	Location
Angulations	Right Parietal
Rotations	Left Parietal
Collisions	Right Pre-frontal
Enlargement	Right Pre-frontal
Perseverations	Right Pre-frontal

Figure 21.1 Cerebral Cortical Location Markers

Each type of miscue the young person makes (angulations, rotations, collisions, enlargement, perseverations, etc) suggest an area of the brain wherein there may be trouble. For example, generally speaking, poorly constructed angles (angulation) made by a youngster point to possible dysfunction within the right parietal (right rear) portion of the cerebral cortex. A teen who tends to *rotate* figures (rotations) may well possess anomalies within the left parietal (left rear) cortex.

On the other hand, figure **collisions** most often point us in the direction of the right pre-frontal region. The same is true when the child makes his copies very large (enlargement), as well as instances wherein the youngster *perseveres* too much in his drawings (perseverations) – e.g., converting a figure of six horizontal dots into *twelve*.

Trail-Making Test

The Trail-Making Test – Parts A and B – assesses visual-spatial skills, visual-motor skills, and mental flexibility. This test is part of the Halstead-Reitan Battery (Reitan, 1994). For Part **A**, the child performs a connect-the-dots type of procedure – locating an encircled "1" on the page, next finding the encircled "2," then the "3," and so on. Trails A specifically addresses visual scanning skills. A poor performance here requires the rule-out (R/O) of: (1) subtle visual-spatial deficits; (2) mild bradyphrenia (sluggish mental processing); and/or (3) anxiety/reticence. Insofar as cerebral cortical location, Trails A can reveal deficits within the right parietal lobe.

Part **B** measures higher cognitive function in terms of mental flexibility. Like Trails A, Trails B is a connect-the-dots task – locating the encircled "1" on the page, then the encircled "A," next the "2," then the "B," and so on. In this fashion, a youth must shift cognitive *sets*, by way of going back and forth in her mind between numbers and letters. This sort of task serves as a mental obstacle course for the pre-frontal lobes. If a child's score rests within the dysfunctional range, such typically constitutes a bilateral (both left *and* right pre-frontal regions) soft-sign.

For younger children (ages 5-8), I use the Color Form and Progressive Figures Tests – from the Reitan-Indiana Battery (Reitan,

1994) – to assess higher cortical function vis-à-vis their ability to shift cognitive sets back and forth between colors and geometric figures. A poor performance reflects possible cognitive inflexibility. Again, like Trails B, a poor score constitutes a bilateral (both left *and* right) pre-frontal soft-sign.

WISC-III

In Chapter 5, we spoke of the IQ measure **I** prefer – the Wechsler Intelligence Scale for Children – III (Wechsler, 1991). This test breaks out into two portions: (1) Verbal subtests; and (2) Performance subtests. The Verbal section of the test measures a child's verbal acumen, while the Performance portion assesses visual-motor and vis-ual-spatial abilities.

WISC-III Verbal Subtests

The WISC-III Verbal Scale assesses the following:

(1) *Information* – fund of stored knowledge. Children who have impoverished backgrounds will oftentimes score out low on Informa-tion. They simply have not been exposed to the same range of stimuli as youngsters from stable homes. Thus, a low Information score often has *nothing* to do with how bright a maltreated child truly is.

(2) *Similarities* – abstract reasoning skills. Questions here require a kiddo to describe the similarities of particular items (e.g., a tree and a flower – both plants). This subtest gauges a young person's ability to reason abstractly and is especially sensi-

Moreover, for youth hailing from backgrounds of neglect and abuse, [Similarities] constitutes the *single best* predictor of **genetic** VIQ, in my experience.

tive to the left pre-frontal region. Moreover, for youth hailing from backgrounds of neglect and abuse, this section constitutes the *single best* predictor of **genetic** VIQ, in my experience.

(3) *Arithmetic* – numerical operations, as well as auditory attention/concentration. These are basically brief story problems which the child must solve in his head. No pencil or paper is allowed. This subtest is very attention-sensitive. Said another way, kiddoes with ADHD frequently struggle with WISC-III Arithmetic.

Thus, this subtest is one of many individual markers that load onto my ADHD Weighting Scale (see Chapter 7).

(4) *Vocabulary* – overall facility of language expression. Here, the youngster is asked to provide verbal definitions of words (such as "donkey," "statue," "tribe," etc). Weaknesses on the Vocabulary subtest frequently provide a generic left hemispheric soft-sign.

(5) *Comprehension* – common sense reasoning. For example, questions such as, "What would you do if a stranger asked you to get in his car?" are asked. Low scores on this portion frequently point to the left pre-frontal region. Also, Comprehension is considered by me to be the *second best* single estimator of genetic verbal intelligence, when such is among the maltreated child's **higher** scores.

(6) *Digit Span* – auditory attention/distractibility. In this section a youth is asked to repeat strings of digits ("4 – 3 – 7 – 9," etc), initially repeating the digits in the same order after hearing them (Digits Forward). Then in the next section, the youngster is requested to repeat the numbers **backwards** (Digits Backwards). This subtest is another marker of possible ADHD. Consequently, it too is loaded onto the ADHD Weighting Scale.

> ...Kiddoes with ADHD frequently struggle with WISC-III Arithmetic.

WISC-III Performance Subtests

The WISC-III Performance Scale measures the following:

(1) *Picture Completion* – visual attention. Here, the child is asked to look at a series of pictures wherein an important part has been left out (e.g., a horse without a tail, or a door without its knob, etc). This subtest also loads on the ADHD Weighting Scale.

(2) *Coding* – visual attention, with a secondary sensitivity for fine-motor processing speed. The youngster is asked to copy nonsense symbols which have been assigned to Arabic numerals (e.g., "^" to 6; ">" to 4, etc). Coding tests the youth's visual attention/concentration and is another ADHD-sensitive measure.

(3) *Picture Arrangement* – pictorial sequencing. This portion requires the kiddo to put individual pictures from cartoons – all jumbled up – into proper order. This subtest can reveal dysfunction within the right temporal region of the brain.

(4) *Block Design* – complex visual-spatial skills. Block Design asks the youngster to put together colored blocks to make various geometric designs presented her on cards. Problems with Block Design performance often denote right parieto-occipital region anomalies.

(5) *Object Assembly* – also complex visual-spatial skills. Object Assembly utilizes mixed up jig-saw puzzle pieces which the child must then assemble to *make something* (e.g., pieces of an elephant, motor boat, etc). This is another right parieto-occipital marker.

WISC-III Coding – Incidental Learning Test

This is actually a measure of memory, tacked onto the end of the WISC-III Coding subtest (pairing up a nonsense symbol for the digits "1" through "9"). After the Coding portion is administered, the child is asked to recreate from short-term memory (i.e., *incidental* memory) as many of the digit-symbol combinations as possible. It is separated into two parts: (1) Symbol Recall; and (2) Digit Recall (Kaplan, et al, 1999).

Symbol Recall primarily taxes **visual** memory – with the youth provided the digit, wherein he must supply the corresponding figure (e.g., "x" with "3," etc). Symbol Recall is thought to be sensitive, in most persons, to the right hemispheric tertiary region (i.e., the **junction** of the right frontal, right temporal, and right parietal lobes). Thus, when a youngster has difficulty with this procedure, it usually constitutes a soft-sign of dysfunction to the tertiary integration zone of the right cerebral cortex.

When a kiddo bombs Digit Recall, such constitutes a possible marker of dysfunction to the tertiary integration zone of the **left** cerebral cortex.

In contrast, the Digit Recall subtest (also an off-shoot of WISC-III Coding) **reverses** the information from Symbol Recall. In this instance, the child is provided the nonsense figure, and asked to produce the corresponding number (e.g., "7" with "^"). For the majority of persons, Digit Recall is sensitive to the *left* tertiary region (i.e., the junction of the left frontal, left temporal, and left parietal lobes). Hence, when a kiddo bombs this measure, such constitutes a possible marker of dysfunction to the tertiary integration zone of the **left** cerebral cortex.

Woodcock-Johnson Tests of Achievement – Revised

The Woodcock-Johnson – R, as you remember (see Chapter 6), measures a youngster's academic skills (Woodcock, Johnson, 1989). However, this *mini-battery* of tests (unto itself) – combined with the WISC-III IQ Test – gives us a clearer, more accurate picture of a child's **genetic** IQ, than does the IQ test alone. The three areas assessed via the WJ-R consist of: (1) Reading; (2) Writing; and (3) Mathematics.

The **Reading** section of the WJ-R covers: (1) word recognition; (2) reading comprehension; and (3) phonics. Word recognition is simply the ability to decode and recognize **words**. In reading comprehension, the youngster must read an age-appropriate portion of text, and then answer questions about what he has read. Phonics is the old-fashioned skill of sounding out words (in this case, nonsense words such as "weeb," scrab," etc).

The **Writing** portion of the WJ-R tests a child's knowledge of: (1) punctuation/capitalization rules; (2) verbs/nouns/basic grammar; and (3) spelling. The spelling section is similar to spelling tests in school: we call out a word, use it in a sentence, and the youngster writes it down. Writing skills almost always constitute the leanest scores among kiddoes **I** work with.

The **Math** segment is an all-you-can-eat seafood buffet of different types of arithmetic problems – addition, subtraction, multiplication, division, etc. The items start out very simple and become increasingly difficult. The child works all he *can*, with no time limits. In a separate WJ-R subtest, math *story problems* is assessed.

> Writing skills almost always constitute the leanest scores among children I work with.

Reading subtests weaknesses generally point toward deficits within the left pre-frontal as well as left temporo-parietal lobes of the brain. Writing difficulties **also** generally reflect left temporo-parietal compromise. Finally, a lean math performance may indicate problems in any number of brain cortical regions: left pre-frontal, left temporo-parietal, right pre-frontal, and/or right temporo-parietal.

Gray Writing Samples Test

Also discussed in Chapter 6 is the Gray Writing Samples Test (Gray, 1994). This particular test measures written language skills.

The youngster writes paragraphs using standardized pictures as prompts (with younger kiddoes either copying the alphabet, **or** writing letters of the alphabet to dictation).

Neurologic written language LDs (or Language Learning Disorders – LLDs) usually reveal problems within the left tertiary integration region (again, the area in the left hemisphere where the frontal, temporal, and parietal lobes *join* one another). Gray Writing Samples also help greatly in diagnosing Dysgraphia, Spelling Dyspraxia, and/or Dyslexia.

Stroop Color-Word Test

This neuropsychologic exam (Golden, 1978) measures mental acuity as well as visual attention. The Stroop is composed of three parts: (1) Word; (2) Color; and (3) Color-Word. In the Word portion, the youth must read aloud the printed words *red, blue, green*. A poor performance on this section can constitute a marker of Dyslexia, *or* poor visual attention.

For the Color segment, the neuropsychometrist asks the child to name the color of **ink** in a series of three "X"s *(XXX)* – actually **printed** in either *red, blue, or green* ink. This is primarily a *right-*hemispherically driven procedure for most of us – i.e., color identification. Thus, deficits within the Color portion often point to either a right hemispheric compromise, and/or a general bradyphrenia.

Third, in the Color-Word subtest, the kiddo must say aloud the color of the ink the word is printed in, while ignoring what the word actually *says*. For instance, the word *red* is printed in *blue* ink; therefore the correct answer is *blue*. Similarly, *green* is printed in *blue* ink – with the correct answer being *blue*. Multiple errors here suggest a mental inflexibility, most often a pre-frontal lobe short-coming. Such is the effect from forcing the pre-frontal lobes to shift cognitive **sets** ("I see the printed word *red*, but I have to verbally **state** the color of its ink – *blue*").

Youth who do poorly across-the-board on the Stroop (i.e., on all three subtests), often suffer from an overall bradyphrenia (sluggish mental processing). Such can indicate any of the following: (1) a bi-lateral pre-frontal compromise; (2) a multi-focal pattern of brain dys-function, involving many or most regions of the cortex; (3) a severe ADHD; or (4) a depressive disorder.

Reitan-Klove Finger Recognition Test

This test, also off the Halstead-Reitan Battery (Reitan, 1994), measures basic tactile attention/concentration. Here, the child is blind-folded and must identify the fingertip that is touched, solely via tactile sensation. His hands rest on the table, with the pads of the fingertips lightly touched via a pencil. The purpose of this test is to reveal tactile distractibility. A weakness here constitutes a possible marker of ADHD.

Tactile Finger Recognition was originally designed to measure localized parietal lobe dysfunction. That is, among youth who suffer with left or right parietal lobe damage, they will often perform poorly on this test. As with motor function, tactile sensation is subserved contra-laterally. In Eng-lish, this means that a person with right parietal compro-mise will do poorly on tactile sensation to/with the *left* fin-gertips. An indi-vidual with left parietal compromise will get tripped up via tactile sensation to/with the *right* fingertips.

> In my experience, among kiddoes who do not present with identifiable brain *damage* in either the right or left parietal lobes, a **better** usage of the Tactile Finger Recognition Test is in its utility for helping with the diagnosis of ADHD.

In my experience, among kiddoes who do not present with identifiable brain *damage* in either the right or left parietal lobes, a **better** usage of the Tactile Finger Recognition Test is in its utility for helping with the diagnosis of ADHD. That is, these youth, in my experience often have difficulty with this test. It's fairly dry and monotonous; thus, ADHD children have more problems with this than do non-ADHD youngsters. Thus, the FRT serves as an excellent measure of **tactile** attention.

Reitan-Klove Fingertip Number Writing Test

Similarly, Fingertip Number Writing (Reitan, 1994) also assesses tactile attention/concentration. Still blind-folded, the kiddo must identify a number that is traced on his fingertips, one at a time, with a pencil. Again, we are looking for **tactile distractibility**, to assist with ADHD diagnosis. Difficulties in the Finger Recognition Test *or* Fingertip Number Writing Test are recorded on the ADHD Weighting Scale, inasmuch as either or both can contribute data as to the presence or absence of attention-related deficits.

As I say, among purists, both Finger Recognition and Fingertip Number Writing are known to be sensitive to dysfunction within the left and/or right parietal regions of the brain's cortex. However, for such to occur, a child would need to have fairly prominent damage in either the right or left parietal regions. Barring these, I have found both Finger Recognition *and* Fingertip Number Writing to be much more *commonly* effective in helping to diagnose **ADHD**.

Speech Sounds Perception Test

This test, off the Halstead-Reitan Battery (Reitan, 1994), measures: (1) auditory-visual attention/concentration; and (2) phonetic speech analysis. The kiddo listens to an audio-cassette of a very dull/monotone-sounding adult male, articulating various nonsense words (e.g., "freen," "weab," etc). The youngster simultaneously reads the nonsense words on a page, while *Snooze-a-Thon Man* says the words. If the child's miscues are clustered within certain areas of the test, an auditory/visual inattention is probable (and loaded onto the ADHD Weighting Scale). However, if the errors are scattered throughout the test, such is more **likely** indicative of deficits within the realm of a kiddo's **phonics**. Generally, recognition-phonics is sub-served via the left temporal region for most of us.

Thus, Speech Sounds has the capacity to reveal either a phonics-based deficit, **or** a marker of ADHD – based upon how the child's errors are scattered about the 60-item test.

Seashore Rhythm Test

Another portion of the Halstead-Reitan Battery (Reitan, 1994), this procedure measures: (1) auditory attention/concentration; **and** (2) nonverbal acoustic analysis. For this assessment the youngster listens to a series of beeps on a cassette player. He then reports whether a second cluster of beeps is the *same as* or *different from* the first set. Low scores may reveal a CNS/non-verbal auditory processing deficit, and/or an auditory tracking deficit.

Again, we study the scatter-pattern of the errors. If such are littered all over the ocean floor of the 30-item test, then a CNS/non-verbal processing anomaly is suspected. Conversely, if the errors are *bunched* together (e.g., four errors out of the final six items on the test), then an auditory attention/concentration deficit (ADHD fodder) is more likely. Hence, identical to Speech-Sounds Perception, Seashore Rhythm is another test that loads onto the ADHD Weighting Scale. On the other hand – also similar with the Speech

On the other hand... should the errors be found in *pockets* or clusters, we likely are looking at faulty auditory *attention* – rather than poor CNS auditory *processing*.

Sounds Perception Test – should the errors be found in *pockets* or clusters, we likely are looking at faulty auditory *attention* – rather than poor CNS auditory *processing*.

Test of Auditory Discrimination (TAD)

This neuropsychologic test – referred to as the **TAD** – (Goldman, et al, 1970) is another measure of auditory attention/concentration. The child listens to a cassette tape with a very boring woman's voice. The boring woman is saying boring words (e.g., "rake," or "boy"). The youngster must thus listen to the boring lady saying boring words, while he looks at boring pictures. Upon hearing a boring word on tape, the kiddo then selects the accompanying boring picture on a template presented him. Each template contains four pictures. The youth, for example, hears the boring lady say, "Point to *rake*." He must then find the rake among the four options on the template, and simply point to it.

This first section of the TAD is called the *Quiet* subtest. The reason? The child is in a quiet room, with no distractions – simply listening to the boring lady speaking boring words while he looks at boring pictures.

The second portion of the TAD – the *Noise* subtest – is very similar to the *Quiet* subtest. Here, the youngster is again looking at the same boring pictures to the same boring words spoken by the same boring woman. But now, the **order** of the pictures/words are scrambled up from the *Quiet* subtest). The difference between the *Quiet* and the *Noise* subtests is that with the latter, the boring lady is speaking from within a boatload of background noise, similar to what might have been heard during the 1968 *Tet Offensive*.

Seriously, the background noise sounds to be a busy, clangy elementary school cafeteria – replete with an annoying cacophony of voices, chairs rattling, a cash register intermittently jingling, etc. Thus, the child must auditorily *screen out* said auditory gar-**báge**, homing in solely to the boring lady's *voice*.

ADHD youth frequently experience much difficulty with the TAD Noise subtest. Other ADHD youngsters, I have found, have more trouble with the sterility of the TAD **Quiet** subtest, and actually do *better* on the **Noise** portion. Bottom line, the TAD is a great addition to my battery of tests – specifically in helping with the diagnosis of a neurologic ADHD.

Gordon Diagnostic System

This is a measure of **visual** attention/concentration/distractibility – also sensitive to ADHD. As I say, the Gordon (Gordon, 1989) measures *visual* attention, in contradistinction to the TAD, which gauges *auditory* attention.

The Gordon is a white portable computer, about the size of a breadbox. There is approximately a 3 inch x 4 inch red screen in the middle of the computer which flashes numbers. We tell the kiddo anytime a "1" followed by a "9" comes up on the screen, push the large blue button on the front of the computer. In this way, the child's visual attention can be recorded. This section is called the *Vigilance* subtest.

A final portion, the *Distractibility* subtest, is similar to the Vigilance subtest. Here though, the youngster must hit the button whenever he sees the "1" followed by a "9" – but **now**, additional numbers are flashing on the screen, competing for the kiddo's concentration. Thus, similar to the TAD *Noise* subtest (measuring Mark's attentional capacity in the face of *auditory gar-báge*), the Gordon *Distractibility* subtest measures Mark's concentrational capacity in the face of *visual gar-báge*. Like the TAD, I really like what the Gordon brings to the party in terms of helping with ADHD diagnoses.

ADHD Weighting Scale

As I have already stated, an ADHD diagnosis cannot be based on one or two single tests; rather, a valid diagnostic determination in this regard must usually emanate from *multiple* test results – sensitive to

ADHD Weighting Scale

Modality	Weighting
Testing Session	
Fidgets/Impulsivity	2
Motoric Over-Activity	6
Poor Attention	3
School Setting	
Fidgets/Impulsivity	2
Motoric Over-Activity	5
Poor Attention	2
PIC	
ADHD: Elevations ≥ 90	3
Elevations 80-89	2
Littauer	
Primary Sanguine	3
Secondary Sanguine	2
WISC-III	
Arithmetic	1
Digit Span	1
Coding	1
Picture Completion	1
Gordon	
Delay	1
Vigilance	1
Distractibility	1
Commission Errors	3
TAD	
Quiet	2
Distractibility	2
Stroop	
Word	1
Color	1
Color-Word	1
Speech Sounds	
Distractibility	2
Seashore Rhythm	
Distractibility	2
Reitan-Klove Tactile	
Distractibility	1
Distractibility	1

ADHD Weighting Scale Criteria

0	—	12	=	WNL
13	—	16	=	Mild Range
17	—	20	=	Moderate Range
21	—	↑	=	Severe Range

Figure 21.2   ADHD Weighting Scale Criteria

236

auditory, visual, **and** tactile attention/concentration. By using the ADHD Weighting Scale (Gray, 1996), we can get a lock on whether or not ADHD is polluting the seawater. Above is the Weighting Scale I use (in this instance, for ages 9-12).

Selective Verbal Learning Test

This is a word learning task (Reynolds & Bigler, 1994), wherein the young person is read a list of words, to hold in her short-term memory. She then is asked to say back as many of the words as possible. The examiner then repeats the specific words not recalled by the child, giving her another chance to again **say** the words, with the goal being to retrieve all of them. The examiner continues with this process – supplying any missed words – until the youngster can recite all words twice in a row, **or** after eight attempts (whichever comes first).

Again, this is a test of verbal memory. An intact verbal memory should be able to show improvement from trial to trial. This is another test sensitive to the tertiary integration zone (frontal/temporal/parietal junction) of the left hemisphere.

Abstract Visual Memory Test

Here we have a **visual** memory test (Reynolds & Bigler, 1994). For 10 seconds, the child is shown a series of geometric figures, comprised of dots. After each item, the examiner presents the youth with several **similar** geometric patterns. Only one is correct. She must then *pick* the one which is correct, out of the various choices. The test proceeds until the child misses three items (patterns) out of a group of **five**.

Typically, the more intact a child's visual memory system, the more patterns she will be able to recall – from item to item – out of the choices provided. This is a test sensitive to the tertiary integration zone (frontal/temporal/parietal junction) of the *right* hemisphere, for most persons.

Littauer Personality Profile

This profile (Littauer, 1983) gives us a read on a given young person's psychologic temperament. Typically, an individual has a primary and a secondary temperament, derived from four basic personality groups: Sanguine, Choleric, Phlegmatic, and Melancholy. As I mentioned in Chapter 8, this test is comprised of forty questions, answered by the child's parent/adult caretaker(s).

The Littauer gives us insight into a youth's psyche. Dealing with *all* children in the exact same manner – vis-à-vis the matter of discipline, for example – irregardless of her personality

> Dealing with *all* children in the exact same manner…irregardless of her personality *make- up*, disrespects the child's unique character imbued to her by God.

make-up, disrespects the child's unique character imbued to her by God. Plus, it's a wholly **ineffective** way to discipline young people – maltreated or no.

Personality Inventory for Children (PIC)

This objective personality psychometric – known as the PIC – (Lachar, et al, 1981) is filled out by a parent or adult caretaker *on* his/her youth. This instrument assesses a number of clinical dimensions pertinent to childhood psychologic/emotional status. Additionally, the Learning Triad of the PIC constitutes soft-signs of possible LD. Moreover, there is a *Borderline Conditions* scale, as well as a scale sensitive to ADHD.

The PIC also contains measures of what are essentially characterologic/personality disorder traits: Histrionic, and Narcissistic.

The way in which the PIC is interpreted constitutes a real *no-brainer*. Any scale with a T-score to the right-hand side of the vertical line on the graph constitutes a likely area of deviance, or concern. Conversely, any scale resting on the *left-hand* side of the vertical line rests within the normal range.

For example, in Figure 21.3 below, note that of the sixteen clinical scales, **this** child scores out with eleven elevations. Such include: two of the four *Parental Drain* Indices (at T-Scores of 71 and 81 – see explanation below) – as well as all three scales of the Learning Triad (at 87, 88, and 92), Childhood Depression (at 76), Narcissism (at 101), Anxiety/Insecurity (at 71), Borderline Conditions (at 89), and Social Skills (at 75).

> I find the PIC particularly helpful – both in terms of the clinical information it provides – as well as the ease with which I can sit down and show parents...what is going on **internally** with their son or daughter. The visualization, by way of the PIC graph, is very powerful and informative.

I find the PIC particularly helpful – both in terms of the clinical information it provides – as well as the ease with which I can sit down and show parents the test's assessment of what is going on **internally** with their son or daughter. The visualization, by way of the PIC graph, is very powerful and informative. As I say, Figure 21.3 is a sample graph of information gleaned from a kiddo's PIC.

Randolph's Attachment Disorder Questionnaire (RADQ)

Dr. Elizabeth Randolph's Attachment Disorder Questionnaire (RADQ) (Randolph, 1998) is the best single psychometric I've seen for helping to pinpoint RAD. Not only does this instrument provide a diagnostic *cut-off* value, but analyzing the various *items* endorsed by the parents is **also** helpful (e.g., "My child doesn't appear to experience remorse," "My child is a pathologic liar," etc).

PIC

		20	30	40	50	60	70	80	90	100	110	120
T-Scores					Normal Range			Abnormal Range				
L			30									
F	"Parental Drain"						71					
DEF	Indices					63						
ADJ								81				
ACH									87			
IS	Learning Triad								88			
DVL					55				92			
SOM	Histrionics				49							
D	Childhood Depression						76					
FAM	FOO Conflict				47							
DLQ	Narcissism									101		
WDL	Atypical Depression					62			95			
ANX	Anxiety/Insecurity						71					
PSY	Borderline Conditions								89			
HPR	ADHD					65						
SSK	Social Skills						75					
T-Scores		20	30	40	50	60	70	80	90	100	110	120

Figure 21.3   Sample PIC Assessment Profile Results

Thematic Apperception Test–Gray Adaptation (TAT–GA)

The original Thematic Apperception Test, by Dr. Henry Murray (Murray, 1935), is a very old test. It is a series of 8 ½ x 11 inch paintings in which the patient is asked to *look* at the picture, and then make up a story *about* it. The psychologist then gleans various clues about the individual's personality from the stories concocted. For example, themes of depression, interpersonal insecurity, unresolved anger toward authority figures, etc may emerge.

Starting off my career back in 1976, I used the TAT in its original format. As I say, such entails showing a series of pictures with people in them, then asking the youngster to make up a story (beginning, middle, and an end) **to** them.

However, specializing in the pediatric neuropsychology of maltreated youth, I began to experiment with modifications to the old *standard* TAT, to see if I could adapt the test to better answer the questions that both I **and** kiddoes' parents were interested in. The result was the TAT-Gray Adaptation (Gray, 1989).

From the TAT-GA, I am looking at two target areas: (1) how many of the ten pictures/scenarios to which the youth assigns punishment or capture to the **malevolent** person in the *stem-stories* provided him; and (2) the quality of *verbiage* the child produces (whether the content is appropriate or not, whether there is evidence of subtle thought disorder, etc).

> Based upon the correlation between their *hit-rate* and age, a marker of super-ego structure (or, in plain English, the conscience) can emerge.

The **endings** a youth gives to the *stem-stories* produces a percentage score *hit-rate* (i.e., how often the youngster ascribes some sort of punishment to the evil perpetrator contained in each story). Based upon the correlation between their *hit-rate* and age, a marker of super-ego structure (or, in plain English, the *conscience*) can emerge.

Youth with an underdeveloped *conscience* frequently fail to show overt guilt/remorse for at least a portion of their own misdeeds – at home, school, or what **have** you (Gray, et al, 1982). They furthermore can externalize blame onto others until a halibut begins to yodel. However, for most youngsters, the prognosis is good, in my experience, that a full *plate* of *conscience* **for** them *will* develop – generally within 2 to 4 years (when given the opportunity to remain in a stable living environment wherein appropriate consequences for their misdeeds are provided, *and* when afforded an effective **treatment** plan).

Also, as indicated above, the TAT-GA can also snag a subtle thought disorder (see Chapter 9) that may be under the water-line. Further, it may reveal markers of histrionics, depression, denial, and/or psychosexual maladjustment.

Rorschach Inkblot Technique

In my testing, I also use the famous Rorschach Inkblot Test (Exner, 1995). I have found this procedure to be the single best, bar *none*, in picking up Borderline Conditions of Childhood/Adolescence.

The Rorschach originated with a Swiss psychiatrist named Dr. Herman Rorschach back in the late 1920s. It, along with the TAT, is the oldest psychologic test we **have**.

Dr. Rorschach began using the same inkblots we have today as a parlor game. He would invite people over, pass the cards around, and have his friends describe what they see, using their imagination – picking out birds, monsters, butterflies and so forth – **to** the various blots, much akin to what we as children used to do when looking up at clouds in the sky, *seeing* what might be there (cars, a person's profile, an animal, etc).

> Then in the 1970s an American clinical psychologist, Dr. John Exner, decided to take the Rorschach from a *fly-by-the-seat-of-your-pants* test to a *scientific* psychometric instrument.

Then in the 1970s an American clinical psychologist, Dr. John Exner, decided to take the Rorschach from a *fly-by-the-seat-of-your-pants* test to a *scientific* psychometric instrument. He and his colleagues studied thousands of people worldwide in many different cultures to see what *they* saw in these original ten blots utilized by Dr.

Rorschach. Dr. Exner studied normal persons, Schizophrenic persons, criminals, children of all ages – you name the category of person – he **studied** them. The data was then chronicled and systematized – discovering, in essence – what these different diagnostic categories of people tended to see, time and again, among the various ten blots.

Dr. Exner's scoring system is the closest thing to astrophysics that I have found in the field of clinical psychology. Over the years, I discovered that several of his scale calculations were **particularly** helpful in determining whether a child or adolescent suffers from a skewed sense of reality. A youth's responses reveal many *other* aspects of personality structure and emotional functioning, as well.

I need to emphasize that the full Exner scoring system entails slightly under a bazillion various and sundry clinical indices. For eons, I scored up the full Exner enchilada. Over the years via experience, however, I settled in on the thirteen indices shown in Figure 21.4. Such are in addition to the various Exner *Special Scores* (SSs), which in a nutshell shed light on the likelihood that a youngster is or is not beset by a subtle thought disorder.

Along with the PIC, an abbreviated Exner Rorschach scoring system are, hands down, the two richest sources of **personality** data that I glean from a given child/teen's clinical profile.

Four scales (X-, X+, Populars, and M-) reveal how a youth perceives the world – the filter through which he sees his environment and other people. Specifically, when a kiddo scores three out of these four indices within the deviant range, a mild perceptual distortion is very likely. A cusp mild

Along with the PIC, an abbreviated Exner Rorschach scoring system are, hands down, the two richest sources of **personality** data that I glean from a given child/teen's clinical profile.

perceptual distortion is indicated when **two** out of the four are within the deviant range. When *all* **four** Rorschach reality-testing indices rest within the abnormal range, such constitutes more solidified evidence of a mild perceptual distortion for the youngster.

Additional indices of the Exner Rorschach system provide possible markers of subtle thought disorder, narcissism, unresolved anger, depression, anxiety, denial, and psychosexual maladjustment.

Rorschach

X-	= .48**	(>.42 = abnormal range)	Mild Perceptual Distortion
X+	= .33**	(<.42 = abnormal range)	Mild Perceptual Distortion
Populars	= 4	(< 4 = abnormal range)	Mild Perceptual Distortion
M-	= 1	(≥ 2 = abnormal range)	Mild Perceptual Distortion
SS	= 13**	(≥ 10 = abnormal range)	Subtle Thought Disorder
Fr	= 0	(≥ 1 = abnormal range)	Narcissism
AG	= 0	(≥ 3 = abnormal range)	Unresolved Anger
Mor	= 3**	(≥ 3 = abnormal range)	Depression
C′	= 1	(≥ 3 = abnormal range)	Depression
V	= 0	(≥ 1 = abnormal range)	Depression
m	= 6**	(≥ 3 = abnormal range)	Anxiety
Y	= 3**	(≥ 3 = abnormal range)	Anxiety
Sx	= 0	(≥ 3 = abnormal range)	Psychosexual Maladjustment

** Clinically Significant Range

Figure 21.4 Sample Rorschach Inkblot Profile

In the example above, for instance, this 12 year-old young man's Rorschach points to a probability that he suffers from a cusp mild perceptual distortion (two out of four *MPD* indices are within the deviant range), a subtle thought disorder (elevated *SS*), mild depression (elevated Morbid content), and anxiety disturbance (elevated *m* and *Y*). However, one of my cardinal caveats: I never hang my hat on any one test – I would always look for correlation of a **single test's** finding (e.g., the Rorschach) via the PIC, TAT-GA, etc.

Summary

These, then, constitute the tests **I** use in my battery when performing a thorough neuropsychologic exam on a maltreated youth. I have spend the last 22 years+, trying out various tests. Those that seemed to bring something to the table, I kept. Those that in my judgment appeared to contribute nothing but dead-weight, I jettisoned. For example, I learned about a *lot* of tests in graduate school. However, as I matured in the profession, I found, for *me*, that many added **nothing** to my understanding of a child. After all, that *is* the goal, isn't it? – to systematically explore the bottom of a troubled kiddo's lagoon, find whatever gunk is *down* there, bring it up to the surface, and decimate it.

We in the profession of neuropsychology love to play the game of, "**My** Dad is taller than **your** Dad" and "**My** test is better than **your** test." The old Halstead-Reitan versus Luria-Nebraska debates back in the 1980s come to mind. I couldn't **possibly** care less about this. The truth is: some clinicians perform very well by using certain tests – others do very well using *other* tests.

Thus, I fully respect the test choices of other pediatric neuropsychologists. The instruments **they** have chosen work for *them*. The tests I have chosen work for *me*. The only aspect **I** care about is, "Does the 'X-Y-Z Test' *add* anything to my ability to do a better job of scuba work for a given child and his family?" If it does, I keep it and use it. If it doesn't, it's history.

245

Chapter 22

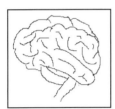

Some Final Thoughts

I'm hoping you've found this book helpful. There is no greater challenge in child-rearing than that which pertains to neglected/ abused youth. For the foster and adoptive parents who take in these youngsters, who love and nurture them, there must be a special place reserved in Heaven.

As we have talked about throughout this book, emotionally suffering young persons often look the same on the outside, above the water-line. But, deep below the surface, they are immensely varied, as diverse as the many species of fish that swim the oceans.

Accordingly, a thorough NP exam, conducted by a well-trained clinician who is savvy with this population of youth, is crucial. Otherwise, we're all playing the diagnostic equivalent of that old 1960's TV show: *What's My Line*?, wherein celebrity panelists attempted to ferret out, via asking questions, which of three contestants was the real Hollywood stunt man, the real ex-fighter pilot, the real deep sea fishermen, etc, etc.

After interviewing all three (the two impostors along with the **authentic** person), the celebrities would cast their ballots for who the *real* individual was. Then, the show's host dramatically asked for the *real deal* to stand up. The panelists were often **wrong**, much to the delight of the studio audience (and those of us playing along from home)!

Well, it's much the same with maltreated youth. Simply by interviewing these kiddoes, it's extremely difficult to tell *What's My **Diagnosis?*** That's where the NP exam comes in. If we don't know the underlying syndromes to treat, we're just stumbling around on a cold, dark ocean floor.

For my part, it's extremely frustrating to see good foster/adoptive parents fumble around with these young persons – albeit doing the best they can – in absence of a thorough NP exam. It's also very frustrating to see **kids** continuing to drown, for lack of a life preserver. I know that a high quality NP evaluation can illuminate the specifics of what these troubled youth are being pulled under by. As such, entire families of neglected/abused children struggle exceedingly more than they **have** to.

Fortunately, we now have the technology to figure out what the underlying root causes of your kiddo's symptoms are. We also have a great deal of resources to improve the quality of human lives. That's the bottom-line message of this book.

It often takes courage and wisdom to step out and do the right thing – for ourselves, as well as for our children. My prayer is if you have taken the time to read this book, you will step out with courage and wisdom. Because, hope abounds!

And if I can help **you** in any way, I will.

The Maltreated Child

Part V

End Notes

Appendix I
Thematic Apperception Test –
Gray Adaptation

Introduction:

"We're going to pretend we're the people who get to make up movies like Steven Spielberg does. I'm going to show you some pictures. For each one, I'll tell you the beginning of the story. But, my stories don't have endings. I need **you** to give an ending to each one of them. However, you have to do this in two minutes or less for each *movie*."

18GF Witch in Disguise

"These women are neighbors. This one here is really a witch in disguise. But no one **knows** she's a witch. She's pretending to be sick. Her next-door neighbor **hears** she's sick and decides she wants to help her by taking some soup over. So, she makes some soup, goes to the house, and rings the doorbell. The witch answers the door, takes the soup, and sets it down. Then, the witch turns around, grabs the woman, and starts **choking** her. She chokes her until she **dies**. What happens next?"

18BM Secret Agent

"This man is a secret agent. He works for the FBI. He's a **good** guy. He's out on a mission looking for foreign spies. One night, he's out late, walking down this dark street, when **suddenly**....a robber comes up behind him and **grabs** him. **Then** what happens?"

17BM   Prisoner Escape

"This man has been in jail a long, long time. He's planning to escape and has been hiding this rope underneath his bed. Well, he pays attention, and one day he notices that when the weekly cleaning people come in, they always leave his window unlocked. So the prisoner talks to a friend of his who is **not** in jail and tells him to meet him in a car about a block away next Tuesday night. Then, when the time comes, he takes the rope, ties it to his bedpost, throws it out the window, and climbs all the way down to escape. What happens next? (Q) What happens with the get-away driver?"

8BM   The Gun

"Here are two boys – about your age, _____ years old. They are outside playing, and start to argue. **This** boy gets so mad; he goes into his house and gets a gun out of his dad's closet and puts bullets in it. He takes it back outside where his friend is. They continue to argue, and finally the boy gets so mad he **shoots** his friend in the stomach. Now, this boy [the victim] is in the hospital, and the doctors are trying to save his life. What happens?"

9BM   Bank Robbery

"All of these guys are bank robbers. They recently stole $250,000 from a bank in Kansas City, and have escaped out of town. Right now they're laying low, being quiet, waiting for the police to stop looking for them. They have a car, and plan on taking the money and driving to Canada. **Then** what happens?"

20   Robber

"This man has just robbed a convenience store, a 7-11. See, he's just stepped out of the store and is standing underneath a street light. You can see it's dark outside and snowing. He is stuffing the $350 he stole from the store into his pocket. Then he takes off running down the street. What happens next?"

251

3GF   Purse Snatcher

"This lady just got home from work. Before she goes into her house, she goes out to check the mail. It's just turned dark. As she's standing by the mailbox, she suddenly feels a hard **slap** on the back of her neck. A man has run by, hit her, and grabs her purse off her shoulder. Well, she then stumbles back into the doorway of her house, where she is **now**. You can see she is still in pain and very upset about all this. Now what happens?"

12M   Haunted House

"This boy moves into a new home in a new neighborhood. On his street is what he thinks is a haunted house. He really, **really** wants to go in and check it out. One day, the boy decides to do just that. He goes into the house and looks around downstairs, but doesn't find anything special.

Then he goes and looks all around upstairs. He enters one of the bedrooms and decides to look under the bed. Know what he sees there? A boot. A **man's** boot. He reaches under the bed and pulls it out. But inside this boot, there is a **foot** – that's been chopped **off**!

Well this obviously **scares** the boy. So he drops the boot and takes off running down the stairs. He tries to run out the front door, but he gets confused and actually opens a **closet** door by mistake. And what is hanging there in the closet? A **skeleton**! Well, this scares him even more. It scares him **so** much that he faints and falls back onto this couch.

See this old creepy man here? Well, he **lives** in the house. Nobody knows it, but he killed his wife and buried her underneath the rose bushes in the back yard 10 years ago. In fact, no one even knows anyone **lives** in the old house. Well, the creepy man has been watching the boy through secret panels in the walls the whole time. And he's none too happy about someone snooping around inside his house.

Now the creepy man is sneaking up on the boy – about to choke him. **Then** what happens?"

9GF   Twin Sisters

"These girls are sisters – twins. They're 18 years-old. This one is Mary (foreground) – the **good** twin. This one is Jane (background) – the **bad** twin. Mary – the good twin – has a boyfriend, but Jane – the bad twin – doesn't. Jane doesn't like this and is very jealous of Mary. Jane thinks if **she** can't have a boyfriend, **Mary** shouldn't have a boyfriend either.

So, Jane – the bad twin – decides she is going to poison Mary's boyfriend one day when Mary is not home. Once Mary goes out, Jane calls Mary's boyfriend and invites him over. He comes over, and Jane gives him a drink with poison in it. He drinks it and **dies**!

Later, Mary hears what happened and hurries home. But she's too late. Now, Mary is standing at the back door. You can also see they live near a beach. See the sand and the water?

Jane – the bad twin – takes off running down the beach with Mary yelling at her, '**Jane**, I know what you **did**! I know you killed my boyfriend! **Stop**!' Then Mary starts running **after** Jane. What happens next?"

15   Ugly Vampire

"This is a mean, old, ugly vampire. He has killed three people in the little town nearby – he sneaks up on them and sucks out their blood. Now, he's standing in an old cemetery, waiting for someone else to come by on the little dirt road there, so he can grab the person and suck out **his** blood, too. What happens?"

Appendix II
Bibliography of Tests –
Gray Neuropsychology Associates, Inc.

Bender, L. *Bender Visual-Motor Gestalt Test.* Los Angeles, California: Western Psychological Services, 1938.

Dunn, L. M., & Dunn L. M. *Peabody Picture Vocabulary Test – Third Revision.* Circle Pines, Minnesota: American Guidance Service, 1997.

Exner, J. E. *A Rorschach Workbook for the Comprehensive System, 4th Ed.* Asheville, North Carolina: Rorschach Workshops, 1995.

Gilliam, J. E. *Gilliam Autism Rating Scale.* Austin, Texas: Pro-Ed, 1995.

Golden, C. *Stroop Color and Word Test.* Wood Dale, Illinois: Stoelting Company, 1978.

Goldman, R., Fristoe, M., & Woodcock, R. W. *Goldman-Fristoe-Woodcock Test of Auditory Discrimination.* Circle Pines, Minnesota: American Guidance Service, 1970.

Gordon, M. *The Gordon Diagnostic System.* DeWitt, New York: Gordon Systems, 1989.

Gray, S. G. *Attention Deficit Hyperactivity Weighting Scale.* Arlington, Texas: Gray Neuropsychology Associates, 1996.

Gray, S. G. *Gray Writing Samples Test.* Arlington, Texas: Gray Neuropsychology Associates, 1994.

Gray, S. G. *Thematic Apperception Test – Gray Adaptation.* Arlington, Texas: Gray Neuropsychology Associates, 1989.

Kaplan, E., Fein, D., Kramer, J., Delis, D., & Morris, R. "Coding – Incidental Learning Test," *Wechsler Intelligence Scale for Children III-PI*. San Antonio, Texas: The Psychological Corporation, Harcourt Brace Jovanovich, 1999.

Lachar, D., Wirt, R. D., Seat, P. D., & Broen, W. E., Jr. *Personality Inventory for Children*. Los Angeles, California: Western Psychological Services, 1981.

Littauer, F. *Littauer Personality Profile*. San Marcos, California: CLASS Book Service, 1983.

Murray, H. A. *Thematic Apperception Test*. Cambridge, Massachusetts: Harvard University Press, 1935.

Randolph, E. *Randolph Attachment Disorder Questionnaire*. Columbia, South Carolina: The Attachment Center Press, 1998.

Reitan, R. "Color-Form Test," *Halstead-Reitan Neuropsychological Battery*. Tempe, Arizona: Reitan Neuropsychology Laboratories, 1994.

Reitan, R. "Finger-Tip Number Writing Perception Test of the Reitan-Klove Sensory-Perceptual Examination," *Halstead-Reitan Neuropsychological Battery*. Tempe, Arizona: Reitan Neuropsychology Laboratories, 1994.

Reitan, R. "Lateral Dominance Examination," *Halstead-Reitan Neuropsychological Battery*. Tempe, Arizona: Reitan Neuropsychology Laboratories, 1994.

Reitan, R. "Progressive Figures Test," *Halstead-Reitan Neuropsychological Battery*. Tempe, Arizona: Reitan Neuropsychology Laboratories, 1994.

Reitan, R. "Seashore Rhythm Test," *Halstead-Reitan Neuropsychological Battery*. Tempe, Arizona: Reitan Neuropsychology Laboratories, 1994.

Reitan, R. "Speech Sounds Perception Test," *Halstead-Reitan Neuropsychological Battery*. Tempe, Arizona: Reitan Neuropsychology Laboratories, 1994.

Reitan, R. "Tactile Finger Recognition Test," *Halstead-Reitan Neuropsychological Battery*. Tempe, Arizona: Reitan Neuropsychology Laboratories, 1994.

Reitan, R. "Trail Making Test," *Halstead-Reitan Neuropsychological Battery*. Tempe, Arizona: Reitan Neuropsychology Laboratories, 1994.

Reynolds, C. R., & Bigler, E. D. "Abstract Visual Memory," *Test of Memory and Learning*. Austin, Texas: Pro-Ed, 1994.

Reynolds, C. R., & Bigler, E. D. "Word Selective Reminding," *Test of Memory and Learning*. Austin, Texas: Pro-Ed, 1994.

Wechsler, D. *Wechsler Intelligence Scale for Children – III*. San Antonio, Texas: The Psychological Corporation Harcourt Brace Jovanovich, 1991.

Woodcock, R. W., & Johnson, M. B. *Woodcock-Johnson Tests of Achievement – Revised: Standard and Supplemental Batteries*. Allen, Texas: DLM Teaching Resources, 1989.

Appendix III
Common Abbreviations/Acronyms

AC – alternating current

AD – Attachment Disorder

ADD – Attention Deficit Disorder

ADHD – Attention Deficit Hyperactivity Disorder

ADHD-WS – Attention Deficit
Hyperactivity Disorder
Weighting Scale

ADL – activities of daily living

aka – also known as

ARD – Admission, Review, and
Dismissal

ATTACh – Association for Treatment and Training in the Attachment of Children

AWOL – absent without leave

BC – Borderline Conditions

BD – Bipolar Disorder

bid – twice per day

BP – Borderline Psychosis

BPA – Borderline Psychosis of
Adolescence

BPC – Borderline Psychosis of
Childhood

BPD – Borderline Personality
Disorder

BSA – Borderline Syndrome of
Adolescence

BSC – Borderline Syndrome of
Childhood

CBD – Childhood Bipolar Disorder

CD – Conduct Disorder

CEO – Chief Executive Officer

CHI – closed head injury

CM – Content Mastery

CNS – Central Nervous System

DBD – Disruptive Behavior Disorder

DC – discontinue

DD – Dysthymic Disorder

DDAVP – Desmopressin

DFO – deviant fantasy operations

DSM-IV – *Diagnostic and Statistical Manual – Edition IV*

DU – dependent underachiever

ED – Emotionally Disturbed

EEG – electroencephalogram

EKG – electrocardiogram

EMDR – Eye Movement Desensitization and Reprocessing

ER – extended release

ETOH – alcohol

FAE – Fetal Alcohol Effects

FAS – Fetal Alcohol Syndrome

FIQ – Full Scale Intelligence

Quotient

FOO – family of origin

G&T – gifted and talented

GAD – Generalized Anxiety Disorder

GARS – Gilliam Autism Rating Scale

GE – grade equivalent

GP – grade placement

GWST – Gray Writing Samples Test

hs – at bedtime

IA – Independent Achiever

ID – Identity Disturbance

IDEA – Individuals with Disability Education Act

IED – Intermittent Explosive Disorder

IEP – Individual Education Plan

IQ – Intelligence Quotient

ISS – in school suspension

LCDC – Licensed Chemical Dependency Counselor

LD – Learning Disability

LiCo – Lithium Carbonate

LLD – Language Learning Disability

LMFT – Licensed Marriage and Family Therapist

LPC – Licensed Professional Counselor

MBD – minimal brain dysfunction

MDD – Major Depressive Disorder

MIA – missing in action

MO – Motivation Plan

MPD – mild perceptual distortion

MR – mentally retarded

MRI – magnetic resonance imaging

NDRI – Norepinephrine-Dopamine Reuptake Inhibitor

NFB – Neurofeedback

NLD – Nonverbal Learning Disorder

NOS – not otherwise specified

OCD – Obsessive-Compulsive Disorder

ODD – Oppositional Defiant Disorder

OHI – Other Health Impaired

OSS – out of school suspension

OT – occupational therapist

PDD – Pervasive Developmental Disorder

PDR – Physicians' Desk Reference

PE – physical examination

PIC – Personality Inventory for Children

PIQ – Performance Scale Intelligence Quotient

PPVT-III – Peabody Picture Vocabulary Test-III

PT – physical therapist

PTIC – Parent Training and Information Center

PTSD – Post-traumatic Stress Disorder

qd – per day

qid – four times a day

RAD – Reactive Attachment Disorder

RADQ – Reactive Attachment Disorder Questionnaire

RAS – Reticular Activating System

R/O – rule out

RTC – residential treatment center

Rx – prescription

SAD – Seasonal Affective Disorder

SARI – Serotonin Antagonist Reuptake Inhibitor

SI – Speech Impaired

SID – Sensory Integration Disorder

SIT – Sensory Integration Training

SMAC – blood tests

SNRI – Selective Norepinephrine Reuptake Inhibitor

SR – sustained release

SS – Special Scores

SSRI – Selective Serotonin Reuptake Inhibitor

STD – subtle thought disorder

TAD – Test of Auditory Discrimination

TAT – Thematic Apperception Test

TAT-GA – Thematic Apperception Test – Gray Adaptation

TBI – traumatic brain injury

TFRT – Tactile Fingertip Recognition Test

tid – three times a day

TMI – too much information

TOP – Tack-On Phenomenon

TVG – Toxic Verbal Gameyness

VIQ – Verbal Scale Intelligence Quotient

WAIS-III – Wechsler Adult Intelligence Scale – 3rd Edition

WISC-III – Wechsler Intelligence Scale for Children – 3rd Edition

WJ-R – Woodcock-Johnson – Revised

WNL – within normal limits

WPPSI-III – Wechsler Preschool and Primary Scale of Intelligence-III

XR – extended release

Appendix IV
Glossary

Abilify – an atypical anti-psychotic medication (used to treat Borderline Conditions/psychoses)

Abstract Visual Memory Test – a standardized visual memory test

Activities of Daily Living (ADL) – necessary, routine, and/or personal care required for day-to-day life

Adderall – a psychostimulant medication (used to treat ADHD)

Adderall XR – a psychostimulant medication, extended release version

ADHD Weighting Scale – an instrument used to diagnose ADHD

Admission, Review, and Dismissal (ARD) – formal process within school systems which provide needed special educational services for students

Affect – demeanor

Ambien – an hypnotic medication (used to treat insomnia)

Amotivation – lack of motivation

Angulations (from the Bender-Gestalt Test) – errors made in copying various angles inherent to geometric figures

Anti-cholinergic – a drug or drug effect that diminishes the effect of acetylcholine, with possible secondary symptoms consisting of dry mouth, constipation, and/or confusion

Anti-convulsants – a class of medications known for stabilizing mood, in addition to their anti-seizure properties

Anti-depressants – a class of medications that can elevate mood (used to treat depression)

Anti-diuretic – medications which reduce the amount of urine the body produces

Anti-enuretics – medications which inhibit the body's production of fluid

Anti-psychotics – also known as neuroleptics; a class of medications used to treat various forms of psychoses

Anxiolytic – anti-anxiety

Anxiolytics – another name for anti-anxiety medications

Ativan – an anxiolytic medication (used to treat anxiety)

Attention Deficit Disorder (ADD) – an older name for the current diagnosis of ADHD

Attention Deficit Hyperactivity Disorder (ADHD) – a diagnosis characterized by difficulty in sustaining attention, forgetfulness, impulsivity. Hyperactivity may or may not be present

Atypical Anti-psychotic – another name for neuroleptic medications (used to treat Borderline Conditions/psychoses)

Auditory Processing Deficit – difficulty in making sense out of various forms of stimuli coming in via the ears

Axons – projections off the nucleus of a neuron cell which carry messages **away** from the cell

Behavior Modification – one of a multitude of different systems which reward a child for exhibiting desired actions

Bender Visual-Motor Gestalt Test – a standardized test measuring visual-motor/spatial skills

Beta-blockers – a class of drugs used to treat ADHD, as well as hypertension

Bilateral – on both sides

Bipolar Disorder (BD) – a syndrome among adults characterized by severe mood swings from elation to deep depression; formerly called Manic-Depressive Illness

Bipolar Disorder of Childhood/Adolescence (BDC/BDA) – a syndrome characterized by extreme irritability, frequent mood swings, and tantrum activity

Borderline Conditions (BC) – a disorder of childhood/adolescence encompassing both Borderline Psychosis **and** Borderline Syndrome

Borderline Personality Disorder (BPD) – a personality disorder wherein severe interpersonal problems, manipulation, irresponsibility, and unstable moods are common

Borderline Psychosis (BP) – an emerging or intermittent struggle with reality via mild perceptual distortion, subtle thought disorder, and/or deviant fantasy operations

Borderline Syndrome – a less severe kissing-cousin to Borderline Psychosis

Bradyphrenia – sluggish mental processing

Brain Stem – that part of the central nervous system leading down from the brain into the spinal column

BuSpar – an anxiolytic medication (used to treat anxiety)

Cardiotoxic – that which is detrimental to the heart

Celexa – an SSRI anti-depressant medication (used to treat depression)

Central Nervous System (CNS) – made up of the brain and spinal cord

Cerebellum – the portion of the brain just above the brainstem which primarily controls balance and motor coordination

Cerebrospinal Fluid – watery substance which helps cushion the brain, as well as the spinal cord

Cerebrum – composed of the pre-frontal, frontal, temporal, parietal, and occipital lobes

Character Pathology – also known as *personality disorders*; a syndrome behaviors which is long-lasting and difficult to change

Choleric – one of the four personality temperaments – decisive, goal-oriented, strong-willed, natural-born leader

Clonidine – a generic Beta-blocker medication (used to treat ADHD symptoms and/or hypertension)

Clozaril – an atypical anti-psychotic medication (used to treat Borderline Conditions/psychoses)

Coding Incidental Learning Test – a standardized visual memory test

Cognition – thought

Cognitive Inflexibility – difficulty shifting from one task to another

Collisions (from the Bender-Gestalt Test) – the drawing of geometric figures such that they collide with one another on the page

Color-Form Test – a standardized test of cognitive flexibility

Co-morbid – two or more simultaneous conditions or diseases

Compulsive Personality Disorder – a personality disorder wherein one has an uncontrollable need/urge for repetitive behaviors

Concerta – a psychostimulant medication (used to treat ADHD symptoms)

Concerta XR – a psychostimulant medication – extended release version

Conduct Disorder (CD) – a behavioral disorder among youth wherein aggression, property destruction, stealing, and blatant disregard for others and/or the law are present

Constriction – stuffing in emotions

Corpus Callosum – a structure joining the two hemispheres of the brain, allowing them to communicate with one another

Cortex – the outer layer of the cerebrum, highly developed in humans

Cortical – referring to the cortex of the brain

Coryza – cold-like (as in headcold)

Cusp – on the border of

Cyclothymia – a cycling of moods similar to adult Bipolar Disorder, but less pronounced

Cylert – a psychostimulant medication (used to treat ADHD symptoms)

DDVAP – an anti-enuretic medication (used to treat wetting)

Dendrite – a branched filament of a neuron which brings electrical impulses (*messages*) **into** a specific brain cell

Depakene – an anti-convulsant medication (used to treat Bipolar Disorder/ Impulse Control Disorders)

Depakote – an anti-convulsant medication (used to treat Bipolar Disorder/ Impulse Control Disorders)

Dependent Personality Disorder – a personality disorder wherein a person is overly dependent and submissive in relationships

Dependent Underachiever (DU) – a youngster, who despite ability, is academically struggling

Depression – a diagnosis in which one can experience any of the following: psycho-motor retardation/agitation, decreased pleasure in activities, social withdrawal, insomnia, fatigue, appetite suppression/enhancement, notions of worthlessness or guilt, inability to concentrate, and suicidal thoughts

Desyrel – an anti-depressant medication with soporific properties (often used to treat insomnia)

Deviant Fantasy Operations (DFO) – the tendency of a youth to tell wild-hare tales, replete with at least a partial *belief* in such

Dexedrine – a psychostimulant medication (used to treat ADHD)

Dextrostat – a combination psychostimulant medication (used to treat ADHD)

Disruptive Behavioral Disorder – a behavioral syndrome among youth characterized by frequent oppositionalism; a less severe kissing-cousin to Oppositional Defiant Disorder

Dopamine – one of several neurotransmitters in the brain

Dyscalculia – extreme difficulty involving computational math skills, often due to LD

Dysgraphia – extreme difficulty involving penmanship, sometimes due to LD

Dyslexia – an LD involving reading, spelling, and/or writing skills

Dyspraxia – extreme difficulty with motor control, often associated with LD

Dysthymia – a chronic form of depression

Effexor – an anti-depressant medication (used to treat depression)

Effexor XR – an anti-depressant medication, extended release version

Elavil – a tricyclic anti-depressant medication (used to treat depression)

Electrocardiograph (EKG) – measurement of heart activity

Electroencephalograph (EEG) – measurement of brain wave activity

Emotionally Disturbed (ED) – a Special Education coding which indicates severe emotional distress/behavior

Encopresis – fecal soiling

Enlargements (from the Bender-Gestalt Test) – the drawing of geometric figures too large

Enuresis – problem controlling urination

Eye Movement Desensitization and Reprocessing (EMDR) – a form of psychotherapy involving directed eye movements, enabling the brain to reprocess past trauma

Facies – general facial appearance

Faux Bonding – false bonding

Florid – full bore

Frontal Lobes – part of the cerebrum, just behind the pre-frontal lobes

Full Scale Intelligence Quotient (FIQ) – the bottom-line score off the Wechsler IQ tests

Generalized Anxiety Disorder (GAD) – a diagnosis characterized by *nonspecific* anxiety, involving the autonomic nervous system

Geodon – an atypical anti-psychotic medication (used to treat Borderline Conditions/psychoses)

Gilliam Autism Rating Scale (GARS) – a standardized test measuring Autism

Gordon Diagnostic System – a standardized test assessing visual attention/concentration

Gray Writing Samples Test (GWST) – a test assessing compositional writing skills

Gustatory – the sense of taste

Halcion – an hypnotic medication (used to treat insomnia)

Haldol – a neuroleptic medication (used to treat various forms of psychoses)

Histrionic Personality Disorder – a personality disorder wherein one displays excessive melodrama, along with emotional suppression/repression

Hit-Rate – number of times a phenomenon occurs

Honeymoon Phase – the period in which a new foster or adoptive child joins a family, with none or very few behavioral problems evident

Hyperactivity – excessive motor movement

Hypomania – a less severe kissing-cousin to mania

Hypnotics – a classification of medications used to treat insomnia

Identity Disturbance – a disorder wherein one does not possess an integrated sense of self

Imipramine – a generic form of the tricyclic anti-depressant, Tofranil

Independent Achiever (IA) – a student who successfully manages his own academic workload

Independent Education Plan (IEP) – an annually reviewed/updated written report via a school system's Special Education department – detailing special services, timelines, and evaluation procedures required by a student with a disability

Individuals with Disabilities Education Act (IDEA) – Federal law requiring states to sufficiently educate any child with a disability of one sort or another

Intermittent Explosive Disorder (IED) – a neurologic syndrome which precipitates rage and/or aggressive episodes

Language Learning Disability (LLD) – an LD confined to reading, spelling, and/or writing

Lateral Dominance Examination – a test for determining right/left brain preference

Learning Disability (LD) – difficulty processing environmental/academic information

Librium – an anxiolytic medication (used to treat anxiety)

Lithium Carbonate (LiCo) – a salt (used as a mood stabilizer to treat Bipolar Disorder)

Littauer Personality Profile – a standardized test assessing human temperament

Luvox – an SSRI anti-depressant medication (used to treat depression)

Magnetic Resonance Imaging (MRI) – allows images of the body to be seen via computer

Major Depressive Disorder (MDD) – the most extreme form of depression

Mania – a highly elevated mood, accompanied by frenzied activity

Manic-Depressive Illness – the old term for Bipolar Disorder

Marker – a *road-sign* frequently characteristic of a specific disorder or disorders

Masked Depression – a type of depression often found in youth with manifestations of oppositionalism and rebellion, wherein classic signs of typical depression such as blunted affect, overt sadness, etc are absent

Medulla Oblongata – part of the brainstem, controlling involuntary actions (such as heart rhythm, respiration, etc)

Melancholic – one of the four personality temperaments – usually described as organized and detail-oriented

Mellaril – a neuroleptic medication (used to treat various forms of psychoses)

Meninges – three thin layers of membranes separating the skull from the brain

Metadate – a psychostimulant medication (used to treat ADHD symptoms)

Methylphenidate – the generic form of Ritalin

Mild Perceptual Distortion (MPD) – the tendency to misinterpret the intentions of others

Minimal Brain Dysfunction (MBD) – an old term indicating mild impairment of brain function

Moban – a neuroleptic medication (used to treat psychoses)

Mood Stabilizer – a psychotropic capable of smoothing out the highs and/or lows of mood

Narcissistic Personality Disorder – a personality disorder characterized by selfishness, extreme stubbornness, and strong sense of entitlement

Navane – a neuroleptic medication (used to treat psychoses)

Neurofeedback (NFB) – measurement/regulation of brain electrical activity

Neuroleptic – another name for anti-psychotic medications

Neuron – brain cells

Neurontin – an anti-convulsant medication (used to treat impulse control disorders)

Neurotransmitters – chemical substances which carry messages between brain cells

Nonverbal Learning Disability (NLD) – an atypical form of LD characterized by deficits in motor coordination, visual-spatial skills, and interpersonal relationships

Norepinephrine – one of several neurotransmitters in the brain

Norepinephrine-Dopamine Reuptake Inhibitor (NDRI) – a type of antidepressant which allows the brain to better utilize the neurotransmitters, Norepinephrine and Dopamine

Obsessive-Compulsive Disorder (OCD) – extreme ritualistic behavior which interferes with daily living

Occipital Lobe – the portion of the brain at the back of the cerebrum, governing vision

Oppositional Defiant Disorder (ODD) – a disorder characterized by highly defiant/hostile behavior; a less severe kissing-cousin to Conduct Disorder

Pamelor – a tricyclic anti-depressant medication (used to treat depression)

Panic Attacks – acute episodes of anxiety often accompanied by increased heart rate, respiration, profuse sweating, and notions of impending doom

Parent Training and Information Center (PTIC) – an agency which helps parents negotiate policies and procedures to ensure the best/most appropriate education for their child

Parietal Lobes – the lobes near the back of the cerebrum, performing a large variety of cognitive functions

Parieto-Occipital Region – area of the cerebrum where the parietal and occipital lobes join

Passive-Aggressive Personality Disorder – a personality disorder characterized by hidden/*under-the-table* aggression, as opposed to **overt** hostility

Paxil – an SSRI anti-depressant medication (used to treat depression)

Peabody Picture Vocabulary Test-III (PPVT-III) – a standardized test measuring receptive language

Performance Scale Intelligence Quotient (PIQ) – a measurement of overall visual-motor/visual-spatial abilities, from the Wechsler IQ tests

Perseverations (from the Bender-Gestalt Test) – excessive *perseverence* involing various geometric figures (e.g., copying a short line of dots all the way to the right-hand edge of the page)

Personality Inventory for Children (PIC) – a standardized test measuring psychologic/emotional status, LD, Borderline Conditions, as well as ADHD

Pervasive Developmental Disorder – a syndrome characterized by a host of concurrent developmental anomalies; a less severe kissing-cousin to Autism

Phlegmatic – one of the four personality temperaments – usually described as *laid back*, sensitive to others, patient, a good listener, shy

Phobias – extreme fears related to specific situations or animals

Polypharmacy – taking excessive/multiple medications

Post-traumatic Stress Disorder (PTSD) – a syndrome in which one re-experiences traumatic event(s) from the past – with accompanying fears, nightmares, and CNS disturbance

Pre-frontal Lobes – the most *forward* portion of the frontal lobes, directly behind the forehead – involved in highly complex cognitive processing

Proprioceptive System – governs the awareness of our body in space/ movement

Prozac – an SSRI anti-depressant medication (used to treat depression)

Psychosis – a severe condition wherein an individual loses touch with reality

Psychostimulants – a classification of medications used to treat ADHD which escalate CNS activity

Psychotropics – medications used for mental health purposes

Randolph Attachment Disorder Questionnaire (RADQ) – a standardized test assessing RAD

Rapid Daily Cycling – frequent shifts back and forth from depression to elation/mania during the course of a day or week

Reactive Attachment Disorder (RAD) – a diagnosis characterized by the inability to interpersonally bond

Referential Speaking – speaking in a praise-worthy manner to another adult about a youth within said youth's ear-shot

Reitan-Klove Fingertip Number Writing Test – a standardized test measuring tactile attention/sensation

Reitan-Klove Tactile Finger Recognition Test – another standardized test measuring tactile attention/sensation

Remeron – an anti-depressant medication (used to treat depression)

Repression – the unconscious *stuffing-in* of painful emotions

Residential Treatment Center (RTC) – a highly structured facility designed for significantly disturbed youth not able to live at home

Restoril – an hypnotic medication (used to treat insomnia)

Reticular Activating System (RAS) – a system of neurons within the brainstem impacting attention, alertness, consciousness, and sleep

Risperdal – an atypical anti-psychotic medication (used to treat Borderline Conditions/psychoses)

Ritalin – a psychostimulant medication (used to treat ADHD symptoms)

Rorschach Inkblot Technique – a projective psychometric test, helpful in diagnosing Borderline Conditions

Rotations (from the Bender-Gestalt Test) – rotating various geometric figures during the process of copying them

Sanguine – one of the four personality types, described as very social, extroverted, and talkative

Schizophrenia – one of *several* forms of psychoses – characterized by extreme interpersonal difficulties, a loss of touch with reality, and thought disorder

Schizotypal Personality Disorder – a personality disorder wherein a person impresses as odd/highly eccentric, which **can** escalate into a florid psychosis under conditions of stress

Seashore Rhythm Test – a standardized test measuring auditory attention/concentration and nonverbal acoustic analysis

Selective Norepinephrine Reuptake Inhibitor (SNRI) – a type of anti-depressant which allows the brain to better utilize the neurotransmitter Norepinephrine

Selective Serotonin Reuptake Inhibitor (SSRI) – a type of anti-depressant which allows the brain to better utilize the neurotransmitter Serotonin

Selective Verbal Learning Test – a standardized verbal learning/memory test

Sensory Integration Disorder (SID) – extreme difficulty in processing information coming in via the senses – auditory, visual, tactile, or vestibular

Sensory Integration Training (SIT) – a specialized form of therapy which helps the brain efficiently organize and process sensory information

Serax – an anxiolytic medication (used to treat anxiety)

Seroquel – an atypical anti-psychotic medication (used to treat Borderline Conditions/psychoses)

Serotonin – one of several neurotransmitters in the brain

Serotonin Antagonist and Reuptake Inhibitor (SARI) – a type of anti-depressant which allows the brain to better utilize the neurotransmitter Serotonin, but different in chemical structure to SSRIs

Serzone – an SARI anti-depressant medication (used to treat depression)

Sinequan – an anti-depressant medication (used to treat depression)

Sociopathic Personality Disorder – a severe character disorder wherein anti-social behavior and lack of conscience abide

Soft-sign – a possible *road sign* of one or more specific disorder or disorders – often used somewhat synonymously with *marker*

Somnolence – sleepiness

Soporific – a medication used to induce sleep

Speech Sounds Perception Test – a standardized test of auditory-visual attention/concentration and phonetic speech analysis

Strattera – an SNRI anti-depressant medication (marketed to treat ADHD symptoms)

Stroop Color-Word Test – a standardized test measuring mental acuity and visual attention

Subtle Thought Disorder (STD) – a mild/intermittent abnormality in one's thought processing

Super-ego Structure – the *conscience*

Suppression – the conscious *stuffing-in* of painful emotions

Synapse – the tiny space between nerve cells in the brain

Tack-On Phenomenon (TOP) – adding one psychotropic after another to a youth, without proper ongoing assessment

Tactile – the sense of touch

Tactile Sensory System – organizes information received via the sense of touch

Tardive Dyskinesia – chronic motor tic disorder as a side-effect of chronic neuroleptic medication usage

Teacher-Parent Conduit – teacher/parent communication

Tegretol – an anti-convulsant medication (used to treat impulse control disorders)

Temporal Lobes – the part of the cerebrum which lies underneath the temples – involved in a host of complex cognitive capabilities

Temporo-parietal lobes – region of the cerebrum encompassing both the temporal and parietal lobes

Tenex – a Beta-blocker medication (used to treat ADHD symptoms and/or Hypertension)

Tertiary Region – the junction of the frontal, temporal, and parietal lobes (on either hemisphere of the brain)

Test of Auditory Discrimination (TAD) – a standardized test measuring auditory attention/concentration

Thematic Apperception Test (TAT) – a projective test developed in the 1930s to measure personality structure

Thematic Apperception Test-Gray Adaptation (TAT-GA) – a test measuring super-ego structure, emotionality, and subtle thought disorder

Thorazine – the very first neuroleptic medication, developed in 1953 (for treatment of psychoses)

Tofranil – a tricyclic anti-depressant medication (used to treat depression)

Topamax – an anti-convulsant medication (used to treat Bipolar/Intermittent Explosive Disorders)

Trail Making Test – a standardized test assessing visual-spatial/visual-motor skills, as well as higher cognition

Traumatic Bonding – a warped psychological connection between two people which, while detrimental to one of the individuals, nonetheless emerges

Trazodone – an anti-depressant medication (frequently used to treat insomnia)

Tricyclic Anti-depressants – the oldest group of anti-depressant medications

Unbonded – no meaningful relationship between two people for whom attachment is otherwise expected

Valium – an anxiolytic medication (used to treat anxiety)

Verbal Scale Intelligence Quotient (VIQ) – a measurement of overall verbal abilities, from the Wechsler IQ tests

Vestibular System – referring to structures within the inner ear interfacing with various brain regions, allowing for physical balance/coordination/equilibrium

Visual-Motor – combining vision with motor skills

Visual-Spatial – combining vision with spatial skills

Wechsler Adult Intelligence Scale-Third Revision (WAIS-III) – a standardized IQ test for adults

Wechsler Intelligence Scale for Children-Third Revision (WISC-III) – a standardized IQ test for children and teens

Wechsler Preschool and Primary Scale of Intelligence-Third Revision (WPPSI-III) – a standardized IQ test for preschool and Kindergarten youngsters

Wellbutrin – an anti-depressant medication (used to treat depression)

Wellbutrin SR – an anti-depressant medication, sustained release (used to treat depression)

Woodcock Johnson-Revised Edition (WJ-R) – a collection of standardized subtests measuring academic skills

Xanax – an anxiolytic medication (used to treat anxiety)

Zoloft – an SSRI anti-depressant medication (used to treat depression)

Zyprexa – an atypical anti-psychotic medication (used to treat Borderline Conditions/psychoses)

Bibliography

Abbott, B., & Costello, L. (1947). *Who's On First?* Abbott and Costello Show.

American Psychiatric Association. (1994). *Diagnostic and Statistical Manual of Mental Disorders: DSM-IV*. Washington DC: American Psychiatric Association.

ATTACh. Association for the Treatment and Training in the Attachment of Children. www.attach.org.

Blue, J. (2000). Cell Phone Therapy. Arlington, Texas: Gray Neuropsychology Associates, Inc.

Blue, J. (2001). *Wit's End*. Arlington, Texas: Gray Neuropsychology Associates, Inc.

Child & Adolescent Bipolar Foundation. (2000). www.bpkids.org.

Cline, F., & Helding, C. (1999). *Can This Child Be Saved? Solutions for Adoptive and Foster Families*. Franksville: World Enterprises, LLC.

Cocco, N., & Sharpe, L. (1993). An Auditory Variant of Eye Movement Desensitization in a Case of Childhood Post-traumatic Stress Disorder. *Journal of Behavior Therapy and Experimental Psychiatry, 24*, 373-377.

Conners, C. K., & Jett, J. (1999). *ADHD: The Latest Assessment and Treatment Strategies*. Kansas City, Missouri: Compact Clinicals.

Cornale, M. (1993). *Personal Communication.*

Dobson, J. (1978). *The Strong-Willed Child*. Wheaton: Tyndale House Publishers.

EEG Spectrum (2003). www.eegspectrum.com.

Federici, R. S. (1998). *Help for the Hopeless Child: A Guide for Families*. Alexandria, Virginia: Ronald S. Federici and Associates.

Gray, S.G. (1993). ADD: A Childhood Epidemic? *Arlington Neuropsychological Associates Digest, 2*, 1.

Gray, S. G. (1996). *Attention Deficit Hyperactivity Weighting Scale*. Arlington, Texas: Gray Neuropsychology Associates, Inc.

Gray, S. G., & Blue, J. (1999). Bland Sandwich Therapy. Arlington, Texas: Gray Neuropsychology Associates, Inc.

Gray, S.G., Hughes, H.H., and Schneider, L.J. (1982). Physiological Responsivity to a Socially Stressful Situation: The Effect of Level of Moral Development. *Psychological Record*, 32, 29-32.

Gray, S.G. (1989). Treating Depression. *Metro-McGee Report: The Stress Digest*, 2, 1-4.

Gray, S.G. (1989). Understanding Post-traumatic Stress Disorder. *Metro-McGee Report: The Stress Digest*, 2, 1-2.

Greenwald, R. (1999). *Eye Movement Desensitization and Reprocessing (EMDR) in Child and Adolescent Psychotherapy.* Northvale, New Jersey: Jason Aronson Publishers.

Hughes, D. (1998). *Building the Bonds of Attachment: Awaking Love in Foster and Adopted Children.* Northvale, New Jersey: Jason Aronson Publishers.

Keck G. C., & Kupecky, R. M. (1998). *Adopting the Hurt Child: Hope for Families with Special-Needs Kids.* Colorado Springs: NavPress Publishing Group.

Keck G. C., & Kupecky, R. M. (2002). *Parenting the Hurt Child: Helping Adoptive Families Heal and Grow.* Colorado Springs: Pinon Press.

Kesey, K. (1962). *One Flew Over the Cuckoo's Nest.* New York: Viking Press.

Kranowitz, C. (1998). *The Out-of-Sync Child.* New York: Skylight Press.

LaHaye, T. (1993). *Spirit-Controlled Temperament.* Wheaton: Tyndale House Publishers.

Littauer, F. (1992). *Personality Plus: How to Understand Others by Understanding Yourself.* Old Tappan: Fleming H. Revell Co.

Lovett, J. (1999). *Small Wonders: Healing Childhood Trauma with EMDR.* New York: The Free Press.

Lubar, J.L., & Lubar, J.O. (1999). Neurofeedback Assessment and Treatment for Attention Deficit/Hyperactivity Disorders (ADD/HD). In J. R. Evans & A. Abarbanel (Eds), *Introduction to Quantitative EEG and Neurotherapy.* New York, NY: Academic.

Mahler, M. S., Ross, J. R., & DeFries, Z. (1949). Clinical Studies in Benign and Malignant Cases of Childhood Psychosis. *American Journal of Orthopsychiatry*, 10, 295-305.

Petti, T., & Vela, R. (1990). Borderline Disorders of Childhood: An Overview. *Journal of the American Academy of Child and Adolescent Psychiatry*, 29, 327-337.

Rimm, S. B. (1990). *Smart Parenting: How to Parent so Children Will Learn.* New York: Crown Publishing.

Rimm, S. B. (1995). *Why Bright Kids Get Poor Grades: And What You Can Do About It.* New York: Crown Publishing.

Rourke, B.P. (1995). *Syndrome of Nonverbal Learning Disabilities: Neurodevelopmental Manifestations.* New York: Guilford Publications, Incorporated.

Shapiro, F. (1989). Efficacy of the Eye Movement Desensitization Procedure in the Treatment of Traumatic Memories. *Journal of Traumatic Stress, 2,* 199-223.

Smalley, G., & Trent, J. (1990). *The Two Sides of Love: What Strengthens Affection, Closeness and Lasting Commitment.* Colorado Springs, Colorado: Focus on the Family.

Sterman, M. B., Macdonald, L.R., & Stone, R.K. (1974). Biofeedback Training of the Sensorimotor EEG Rhythm in Man: Effects on Epilepsy. *Epilepsia*, 15, 395-416.

Sterman M. B. (1996). Physiological Origins and Functional Correlates of EEG Rhythmic Activities: Implications for Self-Regulation. *Biofeedback & Self-Regulation, 21* (1), 3-33.

Thomas, N. (1997). *When Love is Not Enough: A Guide to Parenting Children with RAD – Reactive Attachment Disorder.* Glenwood Springs, Colorado: Families by Design.

Index

Order Form

Fax Orders: fax a copy of this order form to 719/487-1755
Email Orders: gray.matter@mindspring.com
Postal Orders: Gray Neuropsychology Associates, Inc.
    1840 Deer Creek Road, Suite 103, Monument, CO 80132

Please send me:

_____ copies of *The Maltreated Child: Finding What Lurks Beneath* @ $25.00 ea.   _____

_____ copies of *Motivating Marvin: Helping Your Academic Underachiever Succeed in School* @ $25.00 ea.   _____

         6% sales tax (CO residents only):   _____

         Shipping (see below):   _____

       Total Due: _____

Payment:

  ☐ Check   ☐ Visa   ☐ American Express
  ☐ Money Order   ☐ Mastercard   ☐ Discover

Credit card number: _____

Name on card:_____ Exp. Date: _____

Signature: _____

Ship to: _____

         _____

         _____

Shipping Rates:
    Media Mail: $ 3.00 per book (allow 2 to 3 weeks)
    Air Mail: $ 5.00 per book
    Fed Ex: $17.85 per book (guaranteed 2-day delivery)

_____ I would like more information regarding an evaluation for my child/teen.